Profit with Leads!

The #1 Easy-to-Learn, Simple Non-Selling
System for Buying and Closing MLM Leads

By Monte Taylor, Jr.

www.montetaylor.com

THANK YOU!

Thank you for purchasing this book. I'd be truly grateful if you'd take a few minutes to REVIEW this or any of my books on Amazon – your feedback is always welcome.

For access to my free "*Make Prospecting Easy*" audio blog, additional scripts, tips and FREE streaming videos designed to help you get full value from this book, please click or go to the link below to subscribe:

montetaylor.com/profitwithleads-free

Dedicated to those steadfast few who continually strive to improve their people skills – never content unless they are growing, learning and evolving – and who seek out challenges that lead to new possibilities and extraordinary lives.

May you always find your highest and best future!

Acknowledgements

I'd like to thank Brooke Hewlett for inviting me to develop and host several "leads training webinars" for HBB Leads and sister companies. Afterwards she suggested that I write a book, or as she described it, "a workbook for people who want to know exactly what to say and do, so they can be successful when calling home-business or MLM leads."

Brooke generously offered her input – particularly for some of the all-important "getting prepared to call" steps – thanks Brooke!

Loud cheers go out to Rich Niccolls at National Leads who offered several outstanding ideas and suggestions for clarity – thank you Rich!

Special thanks to Lin Wilder at Fast MLM Leads for her very thoughtful input.

A thousand thanks to Tom and Bethany Alkazin whose leadership and generosity of spirit has encouraged countless individuals to "believe in better".

My sincere appreciation (and blessings) goes out to the universal muse, Dr. Joe Vitale, for his remarkable wisdom and insight.

Finally my eternal thanks and love to Penny, my bride of twenty plus years; she is an astounding model for the extraordinary wife, mother and friend.

Table of Contents

INTRODUCTION

Why You Need an Insider's Playbook

I'm going to share my insider playbook with you so you can learn to easily engage and successfully close network marketing "opt-in" leads.

My name is Monte Taylor, and I firmly believe that the vast majority of network marketers fail miserably when it comes to contacting, engaging and closing home business or MLM "opt-in" leads.

Sorry, but it's true – that's why you need an "insider's playbook".

Just to be clear, "opt-in" simply means that someone has responded to an ad or lead capture page, usually on the Internet, has filled out a form and/or spoken with a phone interviewer, and in some way indicated that they are interested in learning more about a home-based business or MLM business opportunity.

Unless they've been well trained, most networkers don't know what to expect, what to do or say to prospects, and after perhaps a few dozen or so unproductive, ineffective, not-so-satisfying calls, they give up and retreat back to working only their "warm market".

And, if they happen to believe they've exhausted their warm market contacts, they may throw up their hands in disgust and quit working their direct selling or network marketing business altogether.

Some give up on their dreams.

My mission is to help save you many, many hours (perhaps hundreds of hours) of wasted time, wasted energy and angst.

My goal is "yuk prevention"! And, if you believe as I do that "wasted time is wasted money" then your insider's playbook will help save you money – maybe even help preserve your dreams.

What You Will Learn

You are going to learn everything you need to know (and do) to successfully prepare, engage, close, and follow up your network marketing leads – and you can handle most of your conversations over the phone!

It doesn't matter how little experience you have. I'm going to show you a simple-to-learn, easy-to-use, and fun-to-execute system that will work for anyone who is willing to invest some focused time – perhaps a few hours – learning, practicing and doing.

As a result of your new skills, I predict you'll also be much more effective "in person" over the phone and in all your presentations.

By the time you've completed this workbook you should be able to pick up the phone and call any network marketing, MLM or "looking for a home-based business" lead and know exactly what you need to do to quickly qualify, build rapport, invite (to preview what you're offering), easily manage any questions or objections, close people to action and follow up effectively.

Can I promise you'll have success with everyone you contact? Of course not.

But I CAN promise you'll learn the exact steps that will give you your best chance to quickly (and appropriately) engage and sell more customers, engage and involve more team members, and you'll experience less frustration and perhaps even find that you enjoy yourself.

Imagine that!

Who Am I And How Can I Help You?

I'm a serial entrepreneur, author, coach and business consultant, and the former CEO of two network-marketing companies; I've enjoyed a wonderful and satisfying career in the Direct Selling industry.

More important than managing companies, I've been a devoted advocate of this industry for over 25 years and personally built teams, numbering in the many tens of thousands, as an independent distributor working in the field.

For the "whatever it's worth" column, I have a Master's degree in business administration (MBA) from the Crummer School of Business at Rollins College and hold Master's level certificates in both Executive Coaching and Business Coaching.

I'm also an adjunct consultant for one of the most respected, hands-on, premier, direct-selling and MLM consulting and coaching organizations in the world, the Sheffield Group. www.sheffieldnet.com

Just to be clear, you don't need any of these kinds of educational or work credentials to be successful at calling leads. Of course, I'm very happy to have completed my formal education, but frankly, it didn't help me one iota when it came to learning how to call and close people.

These are the credentials that made the difference:

(1) Calling thousands of leads until I learned how to do it right, started enjoying it, and began getting positive results. (Boy did I screw up a lot in the beginning.)

(2) Being passionate about coaching and helping others learn how to be effective; for me it is immensely satisfying to be even a small part of people's success.

So What Is The Big Problem?

Throughout my career, I've had the opportunity to read perhaps a hundred or more network marketing training manuals, books and "quick-start guides". I've even helped design and author some of them. Frankly, there are some outstanding company and independent "how-to handbooks" available for anyone who chooses to take advantage of them.

So what's the problem?

Almost all of the workbooks are focused on teaching the new folks how to contact and invite their "warm market". And, speaking frankly, most networkers SHOULD begin by contacting their warm market first.

Today, with rare exceptions, I would never start by teaching a new distributor how to call network marketing or opt-in leads. In my opinion, this is simply too much of a challenge for the novice networker.

Beginners usually don't have the confidence, posture or training required to gain positive traction and results with opt-in leads. They typically don't know enough about their company, the products, the industry as a whole, the compensation plan, handling objections and questions, launching and training new people, and so on.

Am I saying you will need to know all of this before you consider calling opt-in leads?

Not necessarily, but you WILL NEED to have a solid familiarity with your company's products and business-opportunity details, which usually takes several weeks, and sometimes months.

It is much easier to first teach distributors how to contact their "warm market circle-of-influence". In other words – the people they know best.

Back to the big problem

Although the leads you purchase have raised their hand by "opting-in", the contacting, engaging and closing part is still similar to cold-market sales. Most leaders who may have had some success with opt-in leads realize it's not something the average networker can do easily.

Whether they admit it or not, most leaders have watched legions of novice distributors quit – mostly because a few friends or family members rejected their initial invitation. As a rule, this initial rejection experience makes the savvy leaders reluctant to teach opt-in lead calling to their new team members.

Warm market engagement is the norm

For the most part, the overarching "launch your new business mantra" in network marketing is, "contact and engage your warm market, then get them to introduce you to their warm market", and so on. In other words, contact your friends and get them to introduce you to THEIR friends so you can make some NEW friends.

Just to be clear, this "friends contacting friends" plan works so well it has helped build HUGE distribution networks and helped create billion-dollar companies for more than 50 years!

I'm absolutely NOT knocking the "call your friends – then meet their friends" concept. I believe in it and practice it – because it works.

However, with the ongoing explosion of digital sleuthing via Internet search engines and worldwide social networking – millions of people (prospects) are out there surfing and searching for new products, better services, novel ways to earn extra income or replace their current income. Some are even looking to see how they could change careers.

So why not learn how to take advantage of this MASSIVE trend?

Why this Book Could Be Great for Your Business

According to the website, statisticbrain.com, there are over 1.5 billion global Internet users performing 6 billion searches per day, and recent data reports that 72% of global Internet users have researched and purchased products and services online.

What this means is that millions upon millions of people are searching every day for products and services, and some of those are searching for information about profitable, ethical business opportunities.

Legions of searchers are filling out "I'm interested" forms on web-based capture pages; they are "raising their hands" and saying, "O.K. ... Someone tell me more about this."

Simply put: "Circle of influence networking" is an absolutely proven, tried and true business building method, but it is NOT THE ONLY way to meet and engage people who may be looking for what you have to offer.

Savvy network marketers who are committed to building successful businesses may want to seriously consider mastering any logical system that can help them engage and sell more prospects.

And that's exactly what this PROFIT WITH LEADS workbook is all about.

Another reason it's good for business is that the more proficient you become at engaging and closing opt-in leads, the better you will also become at engaging and closing your warm-market prospects. This is a wonderful bonus – the skills are absolutely interchangeable and will quickly help to improve all of your communication and people-selling skills.

You've Completed These Steps, Right?

First, I'm going to assume…

… That you've already found a good company and a product (or service) that you believe in.

Second…

… You've completed your due diligence on the direct selling industry (also sometimes known as the network marketing or MLM industry).

If not, or you want to learn more, go to www.dsa.org and also to http://www.directselling411.com/ where you can get the facts on how to evaluate a company, what to expect from direct selling, the benefits, how to earn income, products you can buy, cthical and legal guidelines, history, and more.

Third…

… You have identified an up-line support person and/or team that's ready, willing and able to help you with any questions or concerns you have about the company's products, services, guarantees, recommended training system, legal requirements, business guidelines, etc.

Fourth…

… You have reviewed the company's recommended "basic training" workbook and/or audios/DVD's etc. (Don't skip this part.)

Fifth and last…

… You are ready to grow your business and accelerate your prospecting efforts by learning how to successfully call, engage and close opt-in leads.

By the way, from now on we'll use the name, "opt-in lead" to mean any lead that represents someone who appears to be interested in a home-based business, home-based income, network marketing or MLM opportunity.

You'll understand more about this once you read Chapter Two: The Scoop on Opt-In Leads.

Later Equals Never

If you're like most people, I'm guessing you want to be sure that get your money's worth from the time and energy you invest here.

So be sure that you understand, "Profit with Leads" is also an interactive workbook, meaning there are some sections where it's important (if not critical) to fill in your personal preparation information and scripts.

Please DO NOT skip these fill-in-the-blank sections with the intent to come back later and fill them out. In my experience coaching thousands of people over the years, "later" usually equals "never".

Filling in the blanks is SO important – please trust me on this point by taking the time to get prepared. This preparation will save you from boatloads of disappointment and frustration.

Some Very Useful Download Tools to Help You

I realize some folks don't like to fill in the blanks by writing in their books.

For this reason, or in case you are reading this book on a Kindle reader, laptop, smart phone or some other electronic device, I've created several COMPLETELY FREE (PDF) "fill-in-the-blanks" documents you can download to your desktop and print if you choose.

Instead of writing in your book, or creating scripts on a note pad, feel free to use these downloadable pages to fill out all your preparation information. That way you can be ready to start making your calls.

In addition to the fill-in-the-blank sections, the FREE downloadable PDF's will have many of my sample scripts to help save you some time. Feel welcome to borrow or adapt these scripts for your personal use.

Go to www.montetaylor.com/profitwithleads-free to download the free documents.

In the next section, I'll give you a very quick tour of the overall workbook, so you know exactly what to expect.

Monte Taylor, Jr.

CHAPTER ONE

A Quick Overview Tour

Whenever I'm driving down the highway, I really appreciate those signs that say, "Airport exit approximately 8 minutes" or "Accident ahead 2 miles - stay in the right lane."

So, **Chapter One** is just what it says: an overview of what's coming – what to expect – a quick overview and tour.

The Inside Scoop: What You Need To Know About Opt-In Leads

In **Chapter Two**, you're going to receive a quick-start primer on leads: What types of leads are available? Where do they come from? How to decide what leads are right for you? How to find a quality, reputable company and avoid the "less than wonderful" companies.

If you've already chosen your leads-supply company and are knowledgeable about leads – good for you! You can skip Chapter Two and go right to Chapter Three.

After reading Chapter Two, you'll know most of what you need to know about selecting and buying leads.

The Single Most Important Pre-Calling Activity!

In **Chapter Three** we'll go over the four critical preparation steps:

1. Gathering your "all about my business" information

2. Establishing your prospect tracking and follow-up system

3. Adopting your master prospector's mindset

4. Creating your prospecting communication plan and scripts

Perhaps 70-80% of your success in calling and closing opt-in leads is based on the quality of your preparation in these four areas.

Good news: It won't take you an enormous amount of time; simply **complete the four important preparation steps,** and you'll be good to go.

How to Be an Objections-Handling Ninja!

In **Chapter Four**, I'll show you a very clever easy-to-learn system that will help you manage any objection or question that comes your way from your prospects. The system is called AVVIS™.

With a little practice, you'll soon be ready to respond and "say the right thing to every prospect." In time, you can become a master at helping people move forward and make better decisions.

The Prospecting Formula for "Super Smart" Networkers

In **Chapter Five,** you'll learn the Super-Smart Prospecting Formula™, the #1, easy-to-learn formula to help you engage and close your prospects.

Once you master super smart prospecting, you will have acquired some very powerful skills, and you can begin to enjoy the process of ethically and appropriately turning prospects into willing customers … or into willing members of your sales team

Bonus Prospecting and Persuasion Nuggets

Chapter Six has a few extra special goodies for you.

- You'll learn a proven, time-tested closing question and technique designed to help uncover your prospect's hidden or unexpressed objections, so you know what to do or say next.

- You'll learn a powerful "imagine forward" presentation exercise that can help engage and inspire your prospects or your audience.

- You'll learn a simple communication strategy that will encourage people to make decisions and take positive action.

- In this chapter, you'll also learn an exercise that will enable you to create positive conversations and can help you influence people – with integrity.

- Finally, we'll close with some suggestions for how you can continue growing and mastering your skills.

So let's get started.

Monte Taylor, Jr.

CHAPTER TWO

The Scoop on Opt-In Leads

What Are They? Where Do They Come From?

The vast majority (perhaps 95%) of all network marketing and home-based business leads are generated over the Internet.

The reason is simple: the Internet is the most cost-effective way of generating leads and is the place where most folks go to do their research when they're looking for an income opportunity, business opportunity, or a job.

A smaller percentage of leads are generated from people who have responded to radio-commercials, newspaper and magazine ads, or post cards. In rare cases, a company or individual will sell their subscriber list (of network marketers or biz-op searchers) to a leads company.

Exactly Who Is "The Lead?"

More often than not, the lead is a person (let's call them a prospect) surfing the Internet and checking out their options for ways to make some extra income.

This person is not always specifically focused on making more money until they come across an online income opportunity, and they decide to click through and check it out.

A good example of this is Facebook, where you may notice one of the little ads (currently on the right of your screen) and for some reason (usually an interesting headline) it catches your attention, so you click on it.

Here's what happens:

1. The person checks out an interesting website about a home business or income opportunity

2. They fill out a form and perhaps respond to a few survey questions

3. They input some of their personal contact information and click the "SUBMIT" button

4. They may receive a phone call (from the company that generated the lead) to verify their contact information and further qualify the lead. (More on this later.)

Those are the basics of Internet-based lead generation.

All Leads Are Not Created Equal

I'm sure you already know that some people are different; and some are very, very different. **And so it is with leads.** It's important to accept that some people are just playing around a bit on the web, while others are seriously researching their options.

Some people are **window-shopping**, and others are **ready-to-buy**, and PROFIT WITH LEADS is going to show you exactly how to know the difference quickly.

Why Are You Calling Me?

There can also be MAJOR differences in the way the lead was captured.

Some of the most problematic types of opt-in leads are the "freebie-enticed leads", or what are known in the lead generation business as "incentivized leads".

Incentivized leads can come from contests, free-offer or sweepstake websites that promise a chance to win free electronics, TV's or luxury cruises, free iPads and gift card offers, free magazines or luxury vacation offers.

All the web-surfer has to do is enter their contact information (email, phone, address, etc.) and/or fill out a form, and they are "guaranteed a chance to win".

Also in this category are "free trial offer" leads. The web-surfer comes across a free trial for a product in exchange for their contact information.

Sometimes the company that gathered the incentivized leads decides to sell this list as "business opportunity seekers" even though the unsuspecting "subscriber" had no idea they were about to start receiving calls from strangers who want to talk about their product or business opportunity.

Even though the company may have put something about being able to sell their contact information in the fine print – most people don't read the fine print.

As you can imagine, incentivized or free-trial offer leads are typically less-than-thrilled to hear from you – and for the most part want to know, "Who gave you my name?" and "Why are you calling me?"

The bad news is, if you don't know how the lead was generated, you can wind up paying $1.00 - $3.00 or more for the opportunity to speak with a very annoyed person whose main objective is to get you off the phone as quickly as possible. And some people aren't very nice about it.

Beware Recycled and Harvested Leads

One of the leads industry's trouble spots is when an unscrupulous lead vendor takes their old or aged leads and

recycles them with newer leads. Then they offer them as fresh leads to unsuspecting buyers.

While there are supposed to be certain "time-stamp" protections in place, there are always companies that find ways to get around the system.

You can expect that recycled leads have been contacted several times already, have decided on a company (or changed their mind) and are typically not very happy about receiving ongoing calls. Recycled leads, if you're going to buy them at all, should be sold as "aged leads" and priced substantially lower than fresh leads.

Think of what you'd be willing to pay for very fresh fish – as opposed to not-so-fresh fish – and you can understand the problem.

Another issue is **harvested leads**.

This is where someone writes a computer program to "crawl the web" with sophisticated software to gather and harvest names, emails, and contact information. They convert this information into lists and sell their **harvested lists** to leads companies.

Most leads vendors don't sell harvested leads, but this problem is certainly something you should be aware of when you are selecting your leads supply partner.

Some companies can get away with harvested leads because many untrained, inexperienced leads buyers give up after making a few calls to bad leads and don't make a stink about it.

Statistics show that between 60-70% of people who buy books never read or finish the book.

Similarly, my guess is that over half of the people that buy leads never complete calling their entire purchased leads list in the first place, and this leaves lots of wiggle room for less-than-honest vendors.

Bottom line: Be sure to choose a leads vendor that **you know you can trust**. I'll give you some specific thoughts on how to do that in a moment.

Just because the leads you purchase have time or a date stamp doesn't insure that the leads are good leads. For example, some very good leads may not have IP addresses available. Again, find a lead vendor you trust and a company you can communicate with.

Different Types of Leads You Can Buy

There are dozens of different kinds of leads available for purchase, and my list isn't meant to be comprehensive. I simply want to help you gain a basic familiarity of what's available.

The good news is that reputable vendor's websites usually do a good job of explaining the types of leads they sell, where and how they were obtained, how and if the lead was verified or interviewed, the costs per lead, and their guarantee.

Real Time Leads

With these leads, as soon the prospect requests information (opts in) from a capture page, their information is delivered to you in "real time". The benefit of this is that you typically aren't calling a prospect that has already talked to a dozen other network marketers, or speaking to someone who requested information so long ago they have forgotten about it.

Be aware that these leads are usually **semi-exclusive** and can be delivered to perhaps one or two other lead buyers at the same time.

There's nothing wrong with this. Just make sure you know what you're buying and that your leads company discloses and/or guarantees how many others receive the same lead.

Also, it's a good practice to limit the number of leads the company is providing you every day. This way, if possible, you can call your leads the same day you receive them. This is called your "daily lead volume" and most companies let you set your volume at a pace that's comfortable for you.

Real Time Local Leads

These leads are the similar in that you receive them shortly after the prospect enters submit, but with real time local leads **you can choose the area code** the lead lives in.

These are great if you prefer to work with people who live or work near you, especially if you prefer to meet with them in person later to qualify, present or train.

Most companies will allow you to choose several area codes, which is a good idea if you live in a large metro area with numerous area code extensions and want a bigger area to choose from.

Real time local leads are usually (but not always) delivered to you with the following information:

- First Name
- Last Name
- Street, City
- State, Zip
- Phone Number
- Email Address

- Date/Time Stamp (the day and time the prospect submitted their information)
- IP Address (Roughly, the location of the digital device, computer, etc., the prospect used to connect to the Opt-in page.)

One challenge with real time local leads is their potential availability. For example, if you select an area code in a small metropolitan area code, there may be a smaller pool of "responding prospects", so you may have to wait several days or longer for your leads to be delivered.

Same Day Interviewed Leads

In addition to filling out and submitting a form, these leads have been contacted by phone to make sure, for example:

- Their contact information is correct
- They are looking for and agree to being contacted about a home business opportunity
- They are 18 years of age or older
- They have time (usually at least 5-10 hours a week) to dedicate to a business opportunity
- They have money (usually between $200-$500) to invest in a home business opportunity

Just to be clear, **same-day** means the same day they were interviewed, not necessarily the same day they originally filled out and submitted their form.

A good company will supply you with the following information on "same day interviewed leads."

- First and Last Name
- Street Address, City, State, Zip
- Phone Number
- Email Address
- The name of the agent who contacted the lead

- Answers to different yes or no questions from the interviewer.
- Date and Time of Interview

Be sure to find out if the interviewed leads your company is offering are "live interviews".

Why? Because most telephone interviewed leads are **not** interviewed at all! Instead, they are verified through an auto dialer and asked to press a button on their telephone to confirm their interest.

Phone dialer "push button" interviews are **not really** interviewed properly in my opinion. Any ten-year-old can press a few buttons on the phone and tell you they want to make an extra $500-$1000 month.

Same-day live interviewed leads are some of the best you can invest in, but are also the most costly. Be sure to find out exactly how your vendor interviews these leads, and make sure you are getting exactly what you want; even better, how you can get a replacement lead if you happen to contact a bad lead.

What you want is a vendor that offers full disclosure on all their leads: what, when, who, how, and how much? **And** you want to choose a company with a "lead replacement" guarantee that's easy to understand and easy to access.

Redirect and Other Kinds of Leads

Real Time Redirect: These leads are delivered straight to your website (if you have one). The idea is that these prospects are more targeted and focused on **your** business, since they have just been redirected to **your site** to watch **your** online movie, read **your** copy, and go through **your** presentation.

Long Form Leads: These leads have responded to more questions online. The long form requires more information and more time, and the leads are, therefore, (supposedly) more qualified, and perhaps more interested.

The list continues:

- Christian Leads – the response form indicates they are Christian
- Female Only Leads – obviously gender-specific leads
- Weight Loss Leads – specifically interested in losing weight
- MLM Leads – they have been informed that the business is network marketing or MLM
- Canadian Leads – Leads that reside in Canada
- Travel Leads – interested in travel opportunities
- Post Card Leads – may have responded from a post card rather than a web capture page

What we've covered here are the most common types of available leads. As you can imagine, the types of leads offerings are many and varied.

Custom Qualified Leads:

One company in particular (fastmlmleads.com) offers leads that are "custom qualified." For example, their follow up personnel will contact specific leads by phone (in advance of your call) to verify and confirm that the leads are open to learning about a "travel related business opportunity" or a "weight loss related" home business opportunity.

The retail leads selling marketplace is quite competitive so be sure and look for opportunities to buy from companies that offer products (leads) that are specific to your business needs.

How Are Your Leads Delivered To You?

Today, most companies offer you a free, password protected "customer back-office portal" so you have control of your leads communications with the company through your personal "Leads Control Panel".

You can use your "Leads Control Panel" to communicate with the company and take advantage of features such as:

- The ability to view/sort your leads
- The ability to purchase additional leads
- The ability to pause, speed up, or slow down your lead delivery frequency
- The ability to change the type of leads you purchase
- The ability to order leads on monthly "auto delivery" (often at additional discounts)
- The ability to request replacement leads
- The ability to report bad leads
- The ability to view your leads order invoice history
- The ability to communicate with the company's customer service
- The ability to access training tutorials (video and audio) and FAQ's

New "leads control panel" features are being added or updated by better companies, so be sure to ask if a demo of the company's leads control panel is available for you to review.

How to Choose a Good Leads Company

My recommendation is that you select three or more companies online, then review and compare their leads descriptions, leads package offerings, introductory/new customer specials, pricing and most of all, their guarantees and **lead replacement guarantees**.

The better companies typically have an abundance of written testimonials from satisfied customers. Feel free to write or call the company and ask if they have a referral list with a few satisfied customers you can interview for a recommendation.

Strictly avoid companies that are selling incentivized leads. Remember, you want to buy qualified business opportunity leads only. This means no incentives were used to entice a prospect to fill out a form or survey, and you are purchasing the rights to contact a real business opportunity seeker.

Some companies will share the links to samples of their leads capture pages so you can get an idea of what a prospect sees before they decide to respond.

If a company's website does not state clearly, "We do not sell incentivized leads" – chances are they are selling incentivized leads.

Unless you're interested in speaking to people who want to know why you're calling and bothering them, you **do not** want to buy incentivized leads

In my opinion, your best bet is to choose a company that offers reasonable live customer service hours (for example: Monday - Friday, 8am to 5pm), and other customer support options such as "live chat" plus responsive email customer service.

The truth is, sometimes you won't know for sure just how responsive the company's customer support is until you give them a call when you have a question or a problem.

It's a competitive marketplace, so you can expect new and better customer-centric features and benefits to be offered by companies that truly want to earn your business.

There are number of excellent leads companies to choose from, but of course I'm not familiar with them all.

Here's a good place to start your research for a reputable provider:

National Leads, a company that's been in business for more than ten years (http://www.national-leads.com)

Network Leads (http://www.networkleads.com), a company that's been in business since 1998

Fast MLM Leads (http://www.fastmlmleads.com/), in business since 1999

HBB Leads (http://hbbleads.com/)

In the past, the companies mentioned above have enjoyed an excellent customer service record.

One final thought: Even with solid, reputable companies, sometimes you're going to get a phone number that's no longer in service or come across leads that swear they didn't request any information.

It just happens at times so accept it and move on – but make sure you're chosen a company with good customer service and one that offers a lead replacement policy you understand.

CHAPTER THREE

Preparation: Big Doors Swing on Small Hinges

This is one of those old sayings – attributed to W. Clement Stone, which is rich and full of meaning. It simply points out that big things often happen as a result of small events.

Many people don't seem to realize how certain behaviors or actions can influence or prevent the big things from happening.

If you want to help grow your business by prospecting leads, be aware that preparation – gathering together everything you'll need – is a very high-leverage activity that can help ensure your eventual success. While it may seem like a little thing, it really is one of those seemingly small hinges that can open big doors for you.

The most important step is to **be prepared** for your calls, and this chapter is designed to make it easy for you to be completely prepared!

Step 1: Gathering Your "All about My Business" Information

By simply filling in the following items with the necessary information about *your* business, you will have paved the way for recruiting success!

Don't worry if you don't have everything on this list. If you can't locate one of these items, be sure to contact your enroller or your company's customer support staff and ask for assistance.

Your business e-mail address: (hint: your company may provide you with a company email account: *yourname@yourcompany.com*, or you can create an email address such as *your.name@gmail.com*)

_____
Your business opportunity sign-up or enrollment link

_____
Your product order link

_____
Your "Watch a Video" - Business Presentation Link

_____
Your "Watch a Video" - Product Description Link

_____
Company Webinar Link

_____
Income Disclosure Statement Link
(Note: Established companies disclose and publish their distributor's average income earnings.)

_____
Other Important Link #1

_____
Other Important Link #2

Company or Team Recorded opportunity call:

Phone Number & Access Pin:

_____

Live business opportunity calls:

Date: _____ Time: _____ Phone Number & Pin:

_____

Date: _____ Time: _____ Phone Number & Pin:

_____

Date: _____ Time: _____ Phone Number & Pin:

_____

Your Enroller and/or Up line Contact Information:
You may occasionally want to hold three-way calls or refer leads to your up line to help with answers to specific questions.

Name: _____ Phone: _____

Email: _____

Name: _____ Phone: _____

Email: _____

Name: _____ Phone: _____

Email: _____

Name: _____ Phone: _____

Email: _____

Name: _____ Phone: _____

Email: _____

Did you order your business cards?
Yes / No

Did you personalize your business website with your photo, testimonial, etc.?
Yes / No

Did you add business links to your "About me" section on Facebook, LinkedIn, etc.?
Yes / No

Did you read/review all of your company business materials?
Yes / No

Did you read/review your company website (every page)?
Yes / No

Step 2: Establishing Your Tracking and Follow-Up System

The very next important high-leverage detail you need to prepare is your personal tracking, follow-up and calendar system.

Warning: DO NOT start making calls without having your tracking and calendar system in place. You must be able to keep track of the day and time of your appointments, and to accurately monitor your contacts and follow-ups with prospects.

This might seem obvious, but so many people start out taking notes on a yellow pad or other "fly-by-the-seat-of-your-pants" systems, which are typically not effective.

Find a system that works for you. I happen to use Planner Pad Executive because it works for me. I've tried dozens of electronic device systems and learned (at least for me) that I'm faster, more effective, and can look forward or backward to easily review months of details and information.

Go to www.plannerpads.com and take a look. The company offers a reasonably priced, well-organized system, in my humble opinion. And no, I don't receive an affiliate fee or have an interest in the company.

It can also be a good idea to research Amazon for OFFICE PRODUCTS/PLANNERS AND ORGANIZERS, or go to your favorite office supply store and get a system that allows you to follow up and track every activity you do with your prospects – plus be able to keep it in one place – with or without electricity or Internet service.

Being prepared with your tracking, follow-up and calendar system is one of those "big doors swing on small hinges" items – get the little hinges right, or you can forget about opening the big door.

The last thing you want to be asking yourself is, "Now, when was I supposed to call that person back? Or, "When did I speak to them last?" "Did I ever call?"

Following up when you promise is an opportunity for you to begin demonstrating your positive professional character. Missing an appointment or neglecting to follow up is quite revealing when you think about it, and not in a good way.

Online "All-in-One" Lead Management Systems

Some leads vendors are now offering subscription-based, online tracking systems for following, tracking and communicating with your leads.

The benefit of this is that all the prospecting information resides in your personal online dashboard, including the ability to purchase or return leads. I'm currently reviewing a few of these systems. As of this writing, they still seem a bit pricey, but take a look for yourself and see if they offer benefits that are worth the cost to you. A system like this may be more feasible if you're a calling more than a few dozen leads per week and you can justify the cost.

Bottom line: Whatever system you choose for tracking, be sure to have your system in place before you start making your calls.

Step 3: Adopting Your "Master Prospector Mindset"

The third high-leverage step is becoming aware of just how critical it is to have the ideal mindset before you start making contact with prospects.

So many people say, "Okay, let's go," but an important question for you to consider first is, "What is the very best mindset for prospecting?"

Let me explain and suggest you consider a "master prospector's mindset."

Clarity of Intention Mindset

What self-made billionaire do you know who has interviewed thousands of super-successful people and helped launched the careers of dozens more?

That would be Oprah Winfrey …and Oprah says it like this: "Intentions rule the universe – you have to be aware of the power of your intentions."

When prospecting, ask yourself: "Do I have a survival mindset or a contribution mindset?"

When you have a survival mindset, you tend to make everything all about your needs. Your attitude becomes: *"What am I going to get from this person? How can I convince or close this person so I can reach my weekly sales goals? How can I get this person to do what I want?"*

Unless you are running through the woods being chased by a pack of angry wolves, a survival mindset doesn't typically create productive energy and won't set you up for success with prospects. Your prospects will recognize your, "it's all about me" intention, and will tend to be resistant.

When you hold a "contribution mindset," your posture and attitude are more productive. Your attitude is: *"How can I creatively help this person discover what they need or want?" How can I help and guide them?" "How does what I have to offer serve their needs?"*

Contribution, and the intention of helping people creates a collaborative energy and posture – and helps make people more responsive. With a "contribution mindset" you'll tend to encounter much less resistance and infinitely more clarity of thought. You will tend to listen more carefully and need to talk less.

Take The "Conversational Lead" Mindset

I like to call this the **"Abraham hypothesis"**. I've been following and learning from Jay Abraham for almost 30 years – Jay is an outstanding marketer, trainer, coach, and author, and when it comes to working with clients or prospects – he hypothesizes and strongly suggests:

"Most people are silently begging to be led."

My suggestion for you when prospecting, is to trust the Abraham hypothesis: If you're a professional who cares about people, your clients or prospects – then be well-prepared to respectfully take the conversational lead!

Here's the fundamental key to developing the ability to take the lead:

Ask better questions!

If you want a better business and better results with prospects and clients, then you should learn to ask better questions. Take the lead by learning to ask high-quality, well-thought-out, intentional questions.

I'll help you and suggest some high quality questions in the next chapters.

Change of Focus Mindset

In order to have the most productive mindset, be prepared to get your conversational arrows pointed outward by keeping the focus on your prospect. Here's the underlying message you want to convey:

"I'm truly interested in you."

Don't invest your time trying to be interesting. Focus on your prospect's "interestingness". That doesn't mean you need to be impersonal or that you can never share a story about yourself. It simply means to keep your prospect – the other person – at the center of the conversation.

It's a less trusting, less marketing-friendly world. Most people feel they're being taken for a ride, and on some level they realize that, "they don't know what they don't know". Your job is to prove that you understand them and that you're not just trying to sell them something.

If you want to influence people, then **focus on others**. Give people what they want: empathy, attention, connectedness and clarity. Be authentic – that's what people want – and that's what they respond to.

Step 4: Creating Your "Super-Smart" Communication Scripts

The fourth preparation step is creating your scripts and communication plan in advance.

While this will take you a little time, the simple truth is: once you have all your scripts written out, all of your prospecting conversations are going to be much more relaxed. The advance preparation is crucial to your success. You'll enjoy infinitely better results.

The "Leave a First Message" Script

More than half of your calls to prospects won't be answered on your first call, especially if they don't recognize your number; chances are you'll be connected to their answering machine. So be ready with your "Leave a first voice message" script.

I'll share my script with you, so you have the idea. Of course, you can change it or adapt it to your own preferred communication style.

Here's a sample of the first message I leave:

> *"Hi, Mary. This is Monte Taylor from Orlando, Florida, and you asked for information, saying that you had an interest in learning more about our home-based income project."*

> *"I wanted to follow up to help get you all the information you need, and to answer any of your questions. Could you please return my call? (Leave your phone number) I really think you'll like what we have, and I'm looking forward to speaking with you for a few minutes."*

> *"By the way, if I happen to be busy on another call, please leave your phone number and the best time to call you back. Once again, this is Monte Taylor at (my phone number). Have a great day, Mary."*

Now, that may seem like a long first-message script, but it has intention and purpose to it. Let's review.

"Hi, Mary. This is Monte Taylor from Orlando, Florida...."

I'm sending the message that I'm a real person. I want to connect with Mary by using her first name. I'm from a real place. I'm a professional who is following up on her request for information.

> *"You asked for some information, or spoke with one of our agents* (or whatever the case may be on the type of lead that you bought) *saying that you had an interest in learning more about our home-based income project."*

By the way, I typically don't say "business opportunity". I feel it's a little hackneyed and overused. Decide on a descriptive phrase that you're comfortable with. I happen to use, "home-based income project".

> *"I wanted to follow up to get you all the information you need, and to answer any of your questions."*

Here, I'm sending the message to Mary that our call will be all about the information that she needs, and she requested. This is not about me calling to try to talk her into buying something.

> *"Could you please return my call? I really think you'll like what you hear."*

What I'm doing is offering a positive fast-forward message by saying, "*I really think you'll like what you hear.*"

> *"I'm looking forward to speaking with you. Once again, this is Monte Taylor. Have a great day, Mary."*

I'm professional, confident, and looking forward to helping Mary. After leaving thousands of messages, that's my usual "Leave a message" script.

Once again, feel free to adapt your scripts to your own communication style and to fit your situation and "voice". Keep your voice message enthusiastic and inviting, (but not gushy) and let people hear your confidence when you state your name and where you're from.

Give them clear directions:

> *"If I happen to be busy on another call, please leave your phone number and the best time to call you back."*

If you are very comfortable and experienced using the phone, this script may seem a bit simplistic. That may be true, but this script is also very effective. It's designed to set the tone for the forthcoming conversation …and it gets a lot of prospects to call me back.

Now, take a few minutes and write out your own 'leave a first message script". Don't try to memorize something at this point – write it down.

Once again, if you'd rather not mark up or write in your book, or you happen to be reading this on a Kindle or other electronic device, take advantage of the FREE documents (PDFs) you can download to your desktop and use them to write out your scripts before you start making calls.

In addition, the PDF's will have some of MY sample scripts already filled out 'for inspiration' and could help save you some time. If you want to borrow or copy my scripts, you are welcome to do so.

Go to www.montetaylor.com/profitwithleads-free

Write Down Your "Leave a First Message" Script

_____

_____

_____

_____

_____

_____

_____

After you leave your first message, write the prospect's name, phone number, and the time/day of your first phone call in your planner and then preschedule your next call for 2-3 days later. For example, if your first call was on a Wednesday, place your second call the following Friday or Saturday.

The "Leave a Final Message" Script

My personal choice is to stop calling once I've left two messages, and no more. Of course, you decide what's right for you because you made the investment in your leads.

This is my "Final message" script with comments underneath:

> *"Hi, Mary. This is Monte Taylor again, from Orlando, Florida, leaving a second and final message."*

I don't try to be dramatic by saying *"...final message."* I'm simply giving Mary fair warning by letting her know this is my last call – I'm a busy professional and I don't chase people needlessly. Here's the rest of the message: (Notice it's similar to the first message.)

> *"As a reminder, you requested information saying you had an interest in learning more about our home-based income project. I wanted to try you one more time so I could get you all the information you need and answer any of your questions."*

> *"If you're still interested in home-based income, please return my call. I really think you'll like what you see, and I'm looking forward to speaking with you. Once again, leave your name and number. I hope we get to speak soon."*

This message has the same friendly professional tone, with the added phrase, "*…leaving a second and final message.*"

Write Down Your "Leave a Final Message" Script

_____

_____

_____

_____

_____

_____

_____

The "Tried To Reach You" Email Script

After leaving my second and last message, I make a note in my planner (confirming and checking off that I made the second call), and then I send a **single** follow up email to the prospect.

Here is my typical "tried to reach you by phone" email script: (notice it too is very similar to the "Leave a voice message" scripts).

"Hi, Mary,

This is Monte Taylor from Orlando, Florida.

I believe you recently requested information about our exciting and profitable home-based income project.

Just wanted you to know that I've been trying to follow up but unfortunately haven't been able to reach you by phone. The reason I called was to get you any information you might need and answer any of your questions

I'd really like the opportunity to learn more about you and what you're looking for, and of course, to see if our project is right for you.

Mary, would you do me a small favor?

Would you mind responding to this email (or give me a return call) and let me know if you're still looking for some extra income? I'd really appreciate it

If you've already found something else or are no longer interested – no worries. Please just drop me a quick email to let me know so I can take you off our list.

Thanks Mary, I hope we get to meet soon by phone. Please drop me a quick email or leave a phone message either way.

Thanks in advance,
Monte Taylor
(My contact information)

Feel free to be even more creative with your "haven't been able to reach you" email follow up. Some networkers will include a link in the email that invites the prospect to review a streaming opportunity or product video.

Sometimes a well-crafted follow-up email hits just the right chord with prospects, and they might just respond with a return email or phone call.

If you have a physical address for the prospect, you may want to follow up with a postcard.

Some folks like to go ahead and send the prospect an audio CD or DVD, inviting them to review the enclosure and get in touch if they like what they see. Personally, I'm not in favor of sending a "tool" unless I have the prospect's agreement in advance to review the information and give me feedback.

It's entirely up to you: you invested in your lead, so follow up as many times as you feel is reasonable. Usually I leave just two voice messages, send one follow up email, and then I move on to the next prospect.

Write Down Your "Tried To Reach You" Email Script

_____

_____

_____

_____

_____

_____

_____

If you happen to be organized and persistent, here's another idea. Keep a list of prospects who did not respond to any of your calls or emails, and 30 days later send them one more email with the following subject line: Did you ever find what you we're looking for?

The "Did You Ever Find What You We're Looking For?" Email Script

Re: Did you ever find what you we're looking for?

Hi Mary, this is Monte Taylor from Orlando, Florida.

We never did get the chance to meet by phone so I thought I'd send you a quick email to see if you ever found that extra income project you were looking for recently.

If not Mary, would you consider doing me a small favor?

This is a link to a (streaming video, audio, your website, etc.)

Would you please take a few minutes and review this (streaming video, audio, your website) and see if something captures your attention? It could be just what you're looking for.

Here's how you can reach me if you have some interest or any questions.
(Add all your contact information, website, etc.)

It would be great to hear back from you.

"Drip emails" like this are a bit of a long shot when it comes to getting a response, but if you catch people who are still looking, they may get back to you with some renewed interest.

It doesn't cost you anything but a little time to create an email template and send out a communication that you can use again and again– so give it a try.

Note: Please don't send a follow-up email to someone who responded earlier and requested that you remove his or her name from your list. That's spamming – don't be rude!

Now it's time to write out your "Tried to reach you by phone" email scripts or simply copy my example if you prefer.

Write Down Your "Did You Ever Find What You Were Looking For?" Email Script

_____

_____

_____

_____

Your "Live Person" Scripts

Here's how to handle the call if your prospect answers the phone, I suggest you use a similar script, but adjust it for a "Live person call". Notice my comments under each script.

Once I have the prospect on the phone, I'll say something like this:

> *"Hi Mary, I was hoping we could visit for just a few minutes so I could get you all the information you need and answer any of your questions."*

I use "visit" because isn't that what we often like do with our friends or new friends? Then make sure that the **first qualifying question** that comes out of your mouth is this question:

> *"Mary, is this a good time to speak?"*

For a better perspective, remember all the times you were busy and someone called you on the phone – even if you might like to speak with the person, sometimes it's just not convenient.

Your prospect is usually not sitting idly by their phone waiting for your call. It's both professional and respectful to ask, *"Is this a good time to speak?"*

If it's not a convenient time for your prospect, they will say something like, *"No, I'm busy right now,"* or *"I'm just headed out the door."* They may even tell you why they're busy but sometimes they don't. In any case, it's okay – don't take it as a personal rejection.

If they say, *"It's not a good time,"* then you can respond with this statement, followed with a very important qualifying question:

> *"Oh, sorry, this is an inconvenient time. Just a quick question before we reschedule, are you still interested in learning more about home-based income?"*

This is a very, very smart and valuable qualifying question. They may say "yes," or they may say "no."

Let's start with, "yes."

> Prospect*: "Yes, but it's not a good time for me to speak right now."*

Then you respond:

> *"I understand Mary. So we don't have to chase each other, what would be a day and time we could both put down on our calendars? I'll phone you back then."*

Then go ahead and confirm the day and time.

> *"Okay, I have us down for Thursday, 1 p.m., is this still the best phone number to reach you or do you prefer another number?"*

They may give you another number or a mobile number, perhaps. It's a great question.

> *"Okay, Mary. I promise I'll phone you then. … Just one more question; if you were going to estimate the weekly income you'd like to make, what would you say?"*

Isn't that also a smart qualifying question?

> Prospect*: "Oh, I don't know." Or, they might say, "$400 or $500 a week."*

Whatever their number is you respond with,

> *"Great, we have many people earning that level of income, thanks." Then reconfirm the day, time, and appointment.*

Why is it important to ask, *"If you were going to estimate the weekly income you'd like to make, what would you say?"*

Although most of the leads you'll purchase are prequalified, super-smart prospectors continue to probe with qualifying questions, and the response is a great starting place for your next conversation. Be sure to note their response in your tracking planner.

By the way, if you promise someone you're going to call them back at a specific time, then do it. Keep your promises.

Notice I said, *"Okay, Mary. I promise I'll phone you then …"*

Use your tracking and follow-up system to schedule and keep your appointments. You have an excellent opportunity to begin revealing your professional character by keeping your appointments.

Here are some optional questions you may want to consider:

"Mary, just in case something comes up for you, would you like my phone number if you need to change our appointment?"

If they say yes, I suggest you email or text your number to them. It gives you the opportunity to get a mobile number and/or reconfirm their email address.

I like to ask, just in case something does happen and they need to reschedule. I've had prospects phone me with, *"Oops, something came up. Can we reschedule?"* To me it says that they respect their appointments even though they had to reschedule.

Here's another option:

"Would you like me to send you a reminder or confirmation note? I can email or text it to you."

These additional questions are optional. But sending people reminders is thoughtful and smart, plus they give you additional opportunities to connect.

Always look for opportunities to build rapport and connect. That's part of the reason you're sharing your name, and you're sharing where you're from, because it gives you opportunities to perhaps find common ground by sharing information.

You may describe your business as network marketing, party plan, MLM or referral marketing – whatever you name it, we are all "relationship engineers" – our business relies on our ability to build relationships with others.

Connecting and creating rapport are absolutely essential. From the moment you encounter a prospect on the phone or in person you must always begin by first seeking to build rapport.

Here's the feeling, the underlying message you want to give people: "You seem like an interesting person. I'd like to get to know you better."

The "Live Person No Longer Interested Script"

Here's a good example of what to say if you get an *"I'm no longer interested"* response on a live call.

> You: *"Oh, sorry, this is an inconvenient time. Just a quick question before we reschedule, are you still interested in learning more about home-based income?"*
>
> Prospect: *"No, I've changed my mind."*
>
> You: *"I understand and will be happy take you off of our list." Mary, would you mind if ask you one quick questions before we go, so I know what to write down as the reason?*

Sometimes people will just say "no" or hang up. If that happens, I suggest you simply cross them off your list and move on to the next person.

If they tell you that they didn't request any information or didn't fill out a form, then you've come across a bad lead, and most companies will offer you a replacement. Be sure you are familiar with your lead vendor's lead replacement policy BEFORE you make a purchase from the company.

Occasionally people will tell you the reason or reasons why they changed their mind. (I can't possibly list here all the interesting reasons people will give you.)

If they do share why they changed their mind, be sure and first say, "Thank you!" Super-smart professionals don't argue, get irritated or try to convince people.

Occasionally you may sense an opening from their response, and may decide to keep the conversation going a bit longer.

Whenever you feel there's an opening, I'd suggest you implement the AVVIS conversational system, which you'll learn about in Chapter Four.

The "Live Person, Ready To Speak" Script

You know they're ready to speak because you asked the question:

> You: *"Is this a good time to speak?"*

> Prospect: *"Yes, it is."*

> You: *"Great. To begin, could you tell me how much income you'd like to make on a weekly basis?"*

Your "how much…" question is going to open up some very important discussion points once you hear the prospect's answer – it's **absolutely crucial** to the next steps in your conversation.

Let's say your prospect gives you a number. For example, if they say, "*Oh, about $500 a week*," (or whatever their number is) here's your response:

> You: *"Perfect. I believe our business could help you earn that level of income."*

Now, make absolutely sure your response is true. If they throw out a number and you don't have any people in your business earning that level of income, then don't say it if it's not true. In most cases, people will give you a reasonable income number, and you can respond appropriately.

You're really making progress now. Mary has told you "yes" it's a good time to speak. And, "yes," she's interested in a home-based income project, AND she's told you how much money she'd like to earn.

Here's your all-important **linking** question:

> You: *"Mary, would it be worth [10 minutes] of your time to find out how?"*

I've put "10 minutes" in brackets because I don't know how long your introductory presentation is going to take. You may be using a webinar, audio, streaming video, or even a live presentation. So tailor your response to the time it takes for the presentation you're using.

If Mary again says, "Yes," then say something like this:

> You: *"Great. We have an outstanding introductory video (or fill in the blank). I really think you'll enjoy it, and it will help answer many of your questions. Shall we watch it now?"*

> Prospect: *"Sure."*

Now, my recommendation is not to send your prospect to a presentation, but personally guide them to your presentation. If it's an audio presentation, listen to it with them. If it's a streaming video, take them to the website and if possible stay on the phone or online as they review it.

Why? Because when you get this far along in your conversation, you are likely working with a prospect – not a suspect. So if you can, go watch the webinar or streaming video with them or listen to the audio with them.

Again, when you get a "yes," schedule and confirm your introductory presentation immediately, and for or best results, stay with them, lead them by the hand.

Let them know you'll answer any questions or concerns after they review the presentation, and always confirm the next steps in your conversation.

> You: *"Mary, right after we watch the streaming video, let's get back together on the phone. I'm really eager to get your feedback and impressions."*

Whenever possible, avoid giving oral presentations – they're not duplicable. They send the wrong message. If you're always doing a 10-15 minute, "blah, blah, blah," presentation, what you're teaching people is they've got to learn a 10-15 minute, "blah, blah, blah," presentation too.

Use the equivalent of a tool (webinar, audio overview, streaming video, or another person) so the prospect feels, "Oh, I could easily do the same thing."

People Will Surprise You Sometimes

Sometimes you're moving along nicely in the prospecting conversation and the prospect suddenly takes you "off script". For example, you might have just asked, *"Would it be worth 10 minutes of your time to learn how?"* and rather than saying yes or no, they say, *"How much does this cost?"*

What they're often doing is voicing an unexpressed fear or concern. So here's a great response:

> You: *"Mary, that's an important question."* (Validate their question.) *"Do you have concerns about cost?"*

Don't be afraid to help get people's concerns out on the table where you can shine a light on them and perhaps manage or solve them.

If the prospect expresses a concern such as, "*I haven't been working, my budget is tight … I just wanted to know about the cost,*" here's an appropriate response:

> You: *"I have good news. There's always a cost to start a real business, but with our program we have ways to get you started that almost anyone can afford."*

Then continue:

> *"Here's my suggestion, Mary. Let's take a look at the presentation together and we'll go over the small start-up costs – then you decide. You deserve to see what this is all about and decide if it's for you."*
>
> *"Does that sound fair?"* or *""Does that work for you?"*

I believe this response is respectful, authentic, and makes a reasonable and logical suggestion for moving forward. You've helped get their question or concern out on the table and managed it appropriately.

Note: If the start-up cost for your program isn't small, then don't say, "Small start-up costs."

In Chapter Four: How To Become An Objections-Handling Ninja, I'll share a simple system that will help you be ready to manage any question or concern that comes your way.

Your Closing Script

First: What is a CLOSE? And, why DO we close?

You might be thinking, "Well, that's to get the money, right?" "Or to get them into our deal, or to sponsor them, enroll them, sell them product, get them started, etc."

While sponsoring, enrolling, and selling are certainly important end-point objectives, the FIRST REASON that we close is to help people by providing clarity, direction, next steps and a plan.

Super-smart professionals CLOSE because they want the opportunity to get everything out in the open. Like a physician, you can't manage a fever if you don't take the patient's temperature.

Closing helps you address any negatives, issues, potential misunderstandings or concerns that may come back to bite you later on.

Have you ever sponsored someone into your program, and a few weeks later wondered why he or she suddenly disappeared or quit? There may have been something that wasn't completely understood or explained in the beginning. Closing helps you get all the issues and expectations out in the open – it can save time and help prevent disappointment.

In sales, this is sometimes called a "trial close". Don't be afraid of it – it's what professional networkers do. Closing (and what we'll later call "closing to action") is an indispensable prospecting and communication tool.

Here are some closing scripts you can use after your prospect has reviewed your introductory presentation and perhaps asked a few questions. Begin with this:

> You: *"Mary, I'm really interested in your opinion. What did you like best about what you saw, or you heard, (or you experienced)?"*

Next, after you listen to their response, you can begin by summarizing:

> *"Mary, you're looking to make extra income from home, you reviewed our presentation, and you asked some great questions. Mary, I have a question."* (Pause first),

Here's your **closing** question:

> *"Is there anything holding you back or keeping you from getting started with us today?*

That's a great question, and it allows them to open up and talk about whatever is on their mind – and trust me, something's on their mind. I don't know what they're going to say, but learn this question so you can find out what it is. This is a question you can use again and again.

Here's another excellent closing technique: (more details in Chapter Five)

> You: *"Mary, I'm curious. On a scale of 1 to 10, with one being low, and 10 being high, how would you rate your interest in moving forward with us, and creating that weekly income we spoke about?"*

This is a super smart closing question. Learn it and use it often!

By the way, if they respond with five or less, you're probably wasting your time, but you can still can ask your prospect:

> *"Please tell me, what's missing for you? What's holding you back? What else would you need to know in order to move forward and get started? Is there anything I can help you with?*

Now it's time to complete the rest of your preparation scripts.

Write down your "Would It Be Worth (10 minutes) of Your Time" Script

_____

_____

_____

_____

_____

_____

_____

Write Down Your "How Much Does This Cost?" Response/Script

_____

_____

_____

_____

_____

_____

Write Down One or More "Close To Action" Scripts

_____

_____

_____

_____

_____

_____

_____

Good News …You're almost ready To Begin

If you have been diligent about completing all of your of your early preparation scripts – the effort will pay off handsomely once you begin to engage your prospects.

If you're interested in seeing even more sample scripts for connecting, handling objections, closing to action, etc., consider reading, OBJECTIONS HANDLED! - 101 Sample Scripts for Network Marketers. *"Learn To Say the Right Thing to Every Prospect"*

It contains over 180 sample scripts, responses and ideas for answering or resolving perhaps 90% or more of the most common objections you'll hear as a network marketer. **It's** available from Amazon.com as both a Kindle book and in print.

Before you begin using your new scripts …

Sometimes people are going to say no. Sometimes they will change their mind. Occasionally some person in the household filled out a form (or requested information) but the person you're speaking with didn't know anything about it …and thinks you're crazy – it just happens.

When these types of things do occur, just thank the person for their time and move on. Don't badger or annoy people. If they ask you to take them off of your "call list" – do it!

Take a few minutes and familiarize yourself with the regulations in place related to calling people who have decided they don't want to be called.

Go to: http://www.fcc.gov/encyclopedia/do-not-call-list

Also see:

http://www.business.ftc.gov/documents/bus61-can-spam-act-compliance-guide-business

With quality leads, the vast majority of time you will be contacting people who requested the information, so you're not a telemarketer. Having said that, if they ask you not to contact them again, then respect their privacy

Coming Next – Some Powerful New Skills for You!

In the next chapter, "How You Can Become An Objections-Handling Ninja," you'll learn the basics of how to manage almost any question, objection or concern.

For those who take learning new skills seriously, mastering the process of handling objections can save you tons of time and wasted energy – and offer you the tools you need to appropriately move people to action.

Monte Taylor, Jr.

CHAPTER FOUR

How You Can Become an "Objections Handling Ninja"

How Much Time Does It Take?

One of the prevailing beliefs today is that to reasonably master a musical instrument, ballroom dancing or a sport, for example, you can expect to have to practice that activity for a minimum of about 10,000 hours.

Here's some good news: In the next few minutes, **you're going to at least learn the basics** of how to handle and manage almost any objection, question or concern.

If you're willing to invest just a little bit of time to understand, internalize and practice this simple system – you can become quite good at managing those sometimes pesky objections.

Meet AVVIS – Your New Best Friend

Before you learn more about AVVIS, you need to know that in order for your new best friend to help you, you must bring the right INTENTION, ATTITUDE and POSTURE to the relationship.

The reason I say AVVIS can be your new best friend is that AVVIS is all about creating clarity in conversations. AVVIS will help you uncover vague intentions, murky objectives, and will encourage you (and your prospect) to consider new possibilities and clarify the next steps.

AVVIS is designed to bring structure and positive forward movement to your communication and sales endeavors.

AVVIS will help safeguard you from the anguish and disappointment that are the result of ambiguity with people.

What AVVIS requires

Intention: Your overarching intention must be a true willingness to help people. Think of yourself as their guide, a supportive "thinking partner" or concierge.

Attitude: Your attitude is, "I'm your friendly helper. I'm your 3-D glasses to help you see better."

One of the best ways I know to begin creating this attitude is by listening more and speaking less – listen carefully to what your prospect is communicating so you can clearly understand what it is they need or want. Isn't this what you'd expect from an outstanding concierge?

Posture: Your posture is, "I'm a professional; I will take the lead" (in a respectful, caring, deliberate manner) by asking thoughtful questions. You're in charge of offering ideas for next steps and resolution, and suggesting forward-moving steps.

AVVIS is an acronym for **Acknowledge – Validate – Verify – Isolate – Solve**

> Prospect: *"So, is this one of those pyramids?"* Or, *"Is this network marketing?"*

Acknowledge (the question and the person)

> You: *"Mary, I'm so glad you brought this up. Thank you; it's a very important question."*

Validate (the question or statement)

> You continue: *"Mary, smart people are concerned about getting involved with one of those illegal pyramids. The good news is (our company) has a positive 10-year track record. We're a real business – not one of those fly-by-night schemes. Our business is not a pyramid."*

Verify (the question by asking your own question)

> You: *Mary, if you don't mind, tell me …what's your experience with network marketing?"*

> Note: In the example above, you used a clarifying (**verifying**) question to help you understand if this is a real concern, and if so, what's behind the concern.

> (Perhaps Mary tells you about her perceptions, and what she's heard about network marketing from some friends who didn't do very well, etc.)

Isolate (the objection or concern by asking another question)

> You: *Mary, other than your concern about network marketing, is there anything else that's important?"*

> Mary: *"No, that's my biggest worry."*

> Note: Isolating means you are separating the objection to learn if this is the **real objection** or simply something the person has blurted or just tossed out to you.

> **Real objections** are the deal stoppers if not managed correctly.

Solve (this is where you respond and offer a solution)

You: *Mary, you mentioned that your most important concern is that network marketing didn't work out well for some of your friends. Is that right?"*

Mary: *"Yes, several of my friends seemed to fail miserably at it."*

You: *"Mary, if I could **show you** how our business plan is different, and working successfully for thousands of people just like you and me, plus **show you** how people who dedicate just 8-10 hours a week are enjoying substantial incomes, what would you say?"*

Note: You should always make sure you've addressed or 'solved' their concern or objection, and if possible, get the prospect to **acknowledge** that you've solved their concern.

It may be that you have Mary agree to read a short book, listen to a CD, meet some others or watch a streaming video presentation that helps educate her on the company, the industry, or the products, and therefore solves her concern.

Let's look at some more AVVIS examples.

AVVIS in Action

Don't forget, AVVIS is: **Acknowledge – Validate – Verify – Isolate – Solve**

Prospect: *"I just don't think I could sell. I'm uncomfortable and not very good at selling."*

You: *"Jim, I'm so glad you brought this up. I know a lot of people feel the same way. Tell me about some of your experiences with selling."*

Note how in the example above, you were able to **acknowledge**, **validate** and began to **verify** with one simple statement followed by a short question.

Hint: Take a minute to go back and reread my response to Jim's selling objection.

Perhaps Jim shares his selling experiences; which are mostly negative. And, as he tells his story you learn that Jim once worked for a company that didn't provide him with any training and expected Jim just to, "get out there and do the best he could."

Jim felt lost, and hated the feeling that he didn't know what he was doing; he had no idea what to say to get people interested in the company's products and services.

You also learn that Jim volunteers regularly at his children's school, loves working with teachers and other parents to gain consensus for projects and fundraisers, and is passionate about contributing and "simply helping people."

> You: *"Jim, thanks so much for telling me about yourself and sharing what you love, and also what concerns you. Other than what you feel about the selling aspect of our business, do you have any other concerns?*
>
> (That, by the way, is **isolating** the concern, which is the "I" in AVVIS!)
>
> Jim: *"The selling is my biggest concern. And… maybe just about how much time I'd have to have to dedicate to this to be successful."*
>
> (Notice the prospect had brought up a possible time issue, so now you **acknowledge**, **validate** and **verify** this new issue)

You: *"I'm so glad you brought up the subject of time; time is an important concern. Jim, I'm curious. If you had to guess at how much time you might have each week to dedicate to a worthy project, what would you say?"*

(Again with two simple sentences, you're *listening, acknowledging, validating,* and *isolating* the time concern.)

Jim answers, "About 10-12 hours a week. That's about all I have right now."

Presto! Now you SOLVE.

You: *"Jim, on your first point about sales. Here's my question: if you knew for sure that we could train anyone who's willing and coachable, so they were comfortable and effective in just a short time, would that help? Would you be willing to come to our "Easy Selling" seminar next weekend so you can see first-hand how well our trainings work for people like you and me?"*

Prospect: *"Sure, if you think it will work for me."*

You: *"That's perfect! You're going to love it when you see how we simplify the process! And, to address your second important point about time, which I'm glad you brought up … I'm happy to report there is no problem. If you can truly dedicate 10-12 hours a week part-time, and do the things we teach you to do, I believe you can reach your goals."*

"Jim, almost everyone in our business starts out part-time, so (your company) has created systems and trainings that honor and respect your time. Most people, including me, began on a part-time basis, and

we are building significant incomes with just a few dedicated hours a week."

Now, close with a question to make sure you've solved the issues and your prospect is ready to take the next steps and/or get started.

> You: *"Jim, I enjoy your energy and enthusiasm; and your questions have been great. I really feel we could be successful together. Would you like to know the next steps … and how you can get started?"*

If Jim brings up another concern at this point, what do you do?

Easy. Repeat AVVIS: Acknowledge – Validate – Verify – Isolate – Solve

Here's a very important point to remember: **Listening** is the always the very first thing you do to power AVVIS … and after you solve (by offering your solution or solutions) **always close by asking a question** just to make sure you have resolved or managed their issues or concerns.

In the example below, you are asking indirectly, by checking to see if Jim is ready to move forward. If not, Jim will likely bring up another objection or concern.

> You: *"Jim, is there anything else you need to know, or would you like to know the next steps and how we can get started together now?"*

A Quick Recap of Your Ninja System

AVVIS employs and takes appropriate advantage of basic human psychology; it is a simple "people communications" system designed to help you be much more effective, intentional, and authentic whenever you are offering a product or service to others.

To make AVVIS work for you, you must first recognize and accept that ALL people want to be heard, acknowledged and taken seriously.

A good strategy is to imagine that everyone you meet is walking around with a sign above their head that reads, "Please Make Me Feel Important."

Give people exactly what they want and need (to be heard, acknowledged, and taken seriously) by being an attentive listener and letting them know you understand and appreciate their point of view – even if you don't necessarily agree with their opinion or belief.

Guide your prospecting conversations so they are mainly about the other person. Ask questions that demonstrate your interest in who they are and in what they have to say.

Be interested in others rather than trying to be "interesting to others". The magic that occurs when you focus on others is they'll often report that YOU were the one who was very interesting.

AVVIS: Acknowledge – Validate – Verify – Isolate – Solve

Acknowledge and **Validate** – Regardless of the person's reaction (or negative energy, if any) your first response is to thank and acknowledge your prospect for their objection, question or concern:

> *"Thank you Mary. That's a good question … several others have asked the same thing"*

> *"Jim, I'm glad you brought that up; it's an important point."*

Verify – Clarify the objection by asking thoughtful, non-adversarial, non-threatening questions:

"Would you tell me more about your experience with selling?"

"I understand what you said about not having much spare time. Would you tell me more about your time constraints?"

Isolate – Narrow the objection to one main thought so you can focus on finding the solution and resolving their concern:

"Is having your spouse's opinion and agreement your most important concern?"

"Other than the small investment we spoke about, is there anything else that keeps you from getting started tonight?

Solve – Resolve, answer and address their concerns by answering questions, making appropriate statements and offering a direction or perspective to consider.

You: *"I agree that it is very important that your spouse be on board with your decision. Why don't we meet with him tomorrow, show him the video and make sure he knows how excited you are?"*

You: *"And if he agrees, would there be anything stopping you from getting started right away?"*

You: *"Mary, I want you to feel as strongly as I do about our product. Let's get a sample in your hands today so you can experience the benefits and decide for yourself. Does that seem like a good plan to you?"*

You: *"And if you enjoy the product as much as most people, would there be anything stopping you from getting started immediately?"*

Realize that no matter how hard you try, how good you are or how compelling your offer may be, you can't always convince people, or change their beliefs.

Learn to sort – not convince

Sometimes people say, "no." Just accept it graciously. Be committed to continually practicing and improving your "people communication" skills, but then move on to the next person!

As a special bonus for buying Profit with Leads, and for being a super-smart prospector, I've recorded dozens of "Make Prospecting Easy" audios that offer ideas, and techniques for engaging prospects and handling objections.

Just go to my website, www.monteaylor.com/profitwithleads-free

CHAPTER FIVE

The Super-Smart Prospecting Formula

The Super-Smart Prospecting Formula combines seven activities that will make it much easier for you to achieve the outcomes you want (such as acquiring a new customer or team member), AND it will help keep your "people communication" skills on track.

Anyone can benefit from this formula, and it will help make the process of getting new business much more predictable and stress free.

Consistent, effective prospecting is absolutely essential to your future success in network marketing or direct selling. Don't listen to anyone who tells you any different!

The "super smart" formula offers a simple recipe for you to follow – here are the seven ingredients:

1. **CONNECT**
2. **QUALIFY**
3. **INVITE**
4. **INTRODUCE**
5. **MANAGE OBJECTIONS**
6. **CLOSE TO ACTION**
7. **FOLLOW UP**

These seven activities are distinct yet still flow together; in many of your conversations they will blend almost seamlessly into each another. For example, you can CONNECT and build rapport with someone and later in the same conversation begin to QUALIFY them.

In a few moments you might INVITE them to review your business or sample a product, and you might hand them a tool to INTRODUCE the opportunity.

At any point in your conversation, you might begin to MANAGE OBJECTIONS or CLOSE TO ACTION and suggest next steps.

The process can take just a few minutes or unfold over several days or weeks.

Take just a minute to review the seven activities that make up the Super-Smart Prospecting recipe:

1. **CONNECT** – To create rapport; a relationship of harmony and mutual understanding; a close connection or trust marked by a feeling of affinity, closeness, or kinship.

2. **QUALIFY** – To prove capable or fit; meet requirements of; to make eligible for, or to determine if something or someone is suitable.

3. **INVITE** – To welcome, suggest, entice, to go after; to ask someone to do something or request to participate.

4. **INTRODUCE** – To present; to make known or to bring before the public; to offer for observation, examination or consideration; to show or display.

5. **MANAGE OBJECTIONS** – To successfully handle, answer, redirect, overcome or respond to a prospect's doubts, opposition, concerns or questions.

6. **CLOSE TO ACTION** – To conclude, complete. To reach an agreement; come to terms.

7. **FOLLOW UP** – To finish to completion; follow through on. To increase the effectiveness or enhance the success of by further action.

Two Critical Skills You Must Know and Use

There are two critical skills that support and empower all successful prospecting:

1. Your ability to LISTEN carefully – without interrupting.

2. Your ability to ASK GOOD QUESTIONS – so you can move your prospect through the communication process and to an outcome.

Of course, the importance of careful LISTENING is common knowledge to most people, **but not necessarily common practice**.

You may have heard the saying, *"If you know something, but you don't use it – then you don't know it."*

Unfortunately, most people don't listen with the intent to understand, but with the intent to reply. Most of us are so busy preparing to speak we don't really hear what was said.

Please **don't be like most people** – commit to becoming a super-smart prospector who listens carefully to what people are saying and then asks great questions to keep the conversation moving forward.

Once you adopt the habit of careful listening, you'll find it's much easier for you to craft thoughtful questions and design an **intentional conversation** that moves quickly through all the steps to a mutually acceptable outcome.

So let's begin with the first ingredient in Super-Smart Prospecting recipe: to CONNECT.

1. CONNECT

(To create rapport, a relationship of harmony and mutual understanding; a close connection or trust marked by feelings of closeness or kinship.)

Network marketing relies on relationship building, so connecting and creating rapport is absolutely essential! From the moment you encounter a prospect on the phone or in person, you must always begin by first seeking opportunities to build rapport and connect.

One of the best ways to quickly capture someone's attention (and "connect") is to engage the person in conversation that focuses directly on him or her.

The message you want to send is: "*You are a very interesting person. I'd like to get to know you better.*"

Examples of Connecting Questions

Here are a few examples of connecting questions, and statements to help you begin conversations. Remember, the goal is to connect, build rapport and to see if you might be able to help someone with your product, service or business opportunity.

"*I'm wondering if you'd tell me more about yourself.*"

"*I'm curious about (*your job, your car, something you said).

"*Please tell me more about your work; it sounds interesting.*"

"*What projects are you're working on right now that you're excited about?*"

"*Would you be willing to tell me the story about how you and Bill met?*"

Rapport is like money: its **value increases dramatically** when you don't have it – when you do have it, **opportunities seem to appear everywhere**.

How Can You Quickly Connect and Gain Rapport?

Listen carefully to people! Use questions to build a bridge of trust and understanding. Be interested in learning about them, their values and their needs.

Look for opportunities to help people gain value with your products or opportunity. Make sure helping people is your highest intention.

It's Easy to Connect with People

Send a clear message with your voice, tone and attitude, that you are absolutely, genuinely delighted to meet them, or if you've already met, you are pleased to see them again.

Don't underestimate how the way you first greet someone has the power to set a positive tone and have a favorable impact.

Most people love to talk about themselves, so ask questions and show that you're interested.

Avoiding the "I'm So Interesting" Trap

All prospectors must be careful not to make the mistake of taking the conversational focus **off of the prospect** and redirecting the conversation so it's now about you.

When you do this, you've fallen into the trap of trying to connect by being **interesting** rather than by being **interested**.

Of course, it's important to CONNECT by sharing values and common interests, but make sure you are communicating your interest **in your prospect** rather than demonstrating how wonderful and interesting YOU are.

Here's a simple example of building the connection, but keeping the conversational focus on the prospect. The secret is to respond and then follow up **with a question**. This keeps the focus where it belongs – which is **not** on you.

Prospect: *"I just moved here from California."*

You*: "Oh, wonderful. I was born and raised in California and still have family there ... What brought you here? ... Do you still have family in California?"*

Again: Focus on being interested – not interesting.

Don't worry. If you show people you are genuinely interested in them – they'll find you VERY interesting!

Once you have built some rapport and connection, you can move on to the next step, which is to QUALIFY

First CONNECT – then QUALIFY people.

2. QUALIFY

When most people think of qualifying, they think of finding out if people have enough money or credit to purchase a product or service.

While money enters into the equation, as a super smart prospector, you want to instead think of qualifying as **discovering** or **identifying** a person's needs, wants or desires so you can creatively link your invitation to the person's self-stated interests or needs, and suggest compelling reasons for them to take a serious look at your product or business.

In short, think of qualifying as a **discovery process**. You are a treasure hunter. You're looking for treasure – once you find the treasure it's much easier to decide what to do with it.

Many of the same questions you use might use to connect and build rapport can also provide valuable information to help you qualify and learn about the person's needs or wants.

Qualifying questions that help you determine someone's interests and need:

"I'm curious…"

"Tell me about…"

"Would you mind if I asked you a question about _____?"

"How satisfied are you with your career right now?"

"How is the economy affecting your business?"

"How do you keep your energy level high?"

"What kind of things do you do to prevent disease?"

"How do you make sure your children (or family) get all the nutrients they need?"

"On a scale of one to ten, how important is your health?"

"When is the last time you and your family took a great vacation together?"

"Do you ever worry about what would happen to your family if you were unable to work?"

"Do you ever feel like you never have enough time to accomplish what you want?"

Once you **discover** that a person is less than satisfied with something in their life, or has a specific need or interest, you are positioned to deliver an invitation that addresses that need or problem and offer some creative solutions.

The Difference between Suspects and Prospects

A very important and timesaving question to ask yourself whenever you are prospecting: "Is the person I'm speaking with a PROSPECT ... or in reality just a SUSPECT?"

Remember: Suspects ARE NOT qualified – prospects ARE qualified.

How do you know which is which? – Qualify the person with questions!

Now that you've connected with someone, built some rapport and have a sense of what is missing in the person's life, you can go to the next step, which is to INVITE.

CONNECT – QUALIFY – then INVITE

3. INVITE

The next step is to INVITE. There are three main objectives of your invitation.

1. To connect or link your invitation to the prospect's pain, needs, wants or desires in a way that suggests or offers a possible solution.

2. To arouse interest and curiosity so they will want to learn about your product or business as soon as possible.

3. To gain a firm commitment or an agreed-upon date or time for the person to meet with you or review any other tool you are providing as an introductory overview.

Once you are confident asking qualifying and inviting questions you can often qualify and invite in the same conversation.

Notice in the example below, you've started with a sincere greeting followed by a compliment and a question. Since the prospect gave you an opening (a need), you can proceed directly to an invitation.

> You: *"Hi Dave, I'm happy we have the chance to meet by phone today, how are you?"*
>
> Dave: *"I'm good, thank you."*
> You: *"Did you say you are working presently?"*
>
> Dave: *"Yes, I'm working at UPS."*
>
> You: *"I hear it's very hard work. Do you still enjoy it?"*
>
> Dave: *"I do, but all the holiday hours are really starting to wear me down. I work more weekends than I'd like …but I really don't have any choice."*
>
> You: *"I understand how difficult it must be always having to work on weekends…"*

(So far you've connected and qualified and discovered a possible area of need (he's always working on weekends). Now you can go directly into your invitation.

Remember: **Whenever possible, tie your invitation to the person's expressed need**. Here are several examples:

> You: *"Let me ask you Dave, if I could show you a profitable business that you could start part-time … and potentially replace your current income after a while*

with no need to ever work weekends, would you be willing to invest 10 minutes to take a serious look?"

You: *"Earlier in our conversation you shared how much the economy is hurting your business right now. There's an online movie I think you'd benefit from seeing. Would you be willing to invest 10 minutes to take a serious look and see if it might be right for you?"*

You: *"Jane, you mentioned several times how painful it's been for you to miss so many of your children's after school and sports events because of your work. I believe I have a possible solution. Would you be open to taking the next steps to see if it might be just what you're looking for?"*

You: *"I hear how challenging your work has been this year. If there were a business you could start part-time from home, and it could later replace your full-time income, would be willing to spend 10 minutes or so to learn more about it?"*

Once again, the most compelling invitations **link** the person's needs or desires to the invitation.

If you have listened well, connected and qualified the person with some great questions – then it's easy to INVITE.

What are you inviting them to do? You are inviting them to look at or review a tool, or watch a presentation designed to INTRODUCE the person to your "possible solution".

CONNECT – QUALIFYING – INVITING, then INTRODUCE your product or opportunity.

4. INTRODUCE

The key to INTRODUCING is to identify one or more of your company's professional tools and allow the tool to do most of the work!

One of the most important things to remember with professional tools is that *you are the messenger, not the message* – think of yourself as the 30-second commercial promoting the upcoming show or movie.

Here are some of the most popular ways to present and introduce your product or business to others using professionally produced tools:

- Audio CD's
- DVD's
- Streaming Media (Audio or Video)
- Your corporate website
- Pre-recorded introductory conference/presentation calls
- Printed materials such as retail catalogs, brochures, PowerPoint presentations, and company branded magazines and other print media
- Webinar presentation

Using professionally produced tools has several advantages:

- Using a tool is more duplicable – it's simple and easy to hand out a tool or direct a prospect to a streaming audio/video link on the Internet.

- It's more time-efficient – you can use the tools to help you sift and sort through prospects to quickly determine those who are truly interested. If your prospect can't review the tool immediately for some reason, they can review the tool when it's convenient. It's sometimes easier for someone to review a tool than it is for him or her to attend a live presentation.

- A professionally produced tool, or webinar is often more credible than a personal presentation – and typically more consistent.

- A prospect can review the introductory tool (such as a streaming video) multiple times if they want – and each time they can learn more or build stronger belief in what you're offering

How to INTRODUCE via "Personal Presentations"

Today, it is so easy to give people a digital overview in the form of streaming video, audio, webinar or DVD, that I typically have the prospect review one of these first, give me their impressions or feedback first, before I suggest the possibility of getting together in person.

I prefer to make the most of our initial phone conversations by going over any information they need – including the costs of getting started or other important details about training or compensation plan.

However, if you purchase local opt-in leads you may decide you prefer to meet your prospects face-to-face for a personal introductory presentation rather than over the phone.

Here are three types of personal presentations

- One-on-One Introductions – this is when you meet personally with a prospect at your home, a coffee shop or any other location that is generally free of distractions. You give your prospect a private overview of your product or opportunity and perhaps support your presentation with professionally produced print media.

- Two-on-One Introductions – this is when you and one of your up-line business partners meet with a prospect in a suitable location or via a conference call. This gives you the opportunity to have an experienced third-party handle the presentation. It also gives you the opportunity "to listen and learn" how an experienced person introduces the business. (By the way, an up-line partner is a person above you in organizational structure and someone who typically can benefit either directly or indirectly from your business success.)

I have a free "how-to guide" for 3-way conference calls entitled, "*Sample Scripts for Outrageously Successful 3-Way Calls*" at, www.montetaylor.com/profitwithleads-free

- Private Business Mixers – This is an opportunity to introduce your business to a small group, perhaps in your home, a country club, a meeting room or any other suitable location.

  You and your up line partner can handle the presentation to your guests and whenever possible support the presentation with professionally produced print or media tools.

The Advantages of Personal Introductions

1. Gives the presenter the opportunity to customize the introduction for the individual.

2. Creates an opportunity to have the person's undivided attention for the length of the presentation and eliminate outside distractions.

3. Creates an opportunity for the person to interact and ask questions after the presentation, and perhaps sample the products.

Setting the Stage with "Pre Introductory Questions"

Here are some questions I like my prospects to consider just before they watch my introductory tool.

> *"Have you ever thought about how important it could be to create a "Plan B" just in case something happened to your current income or your job?"*

> *"Have you ever considered what you would need to do in order to create a substantial secondary income stream … with just part-time effort?"*

> *"Off the top of your head, what would you need to do in your life to create an economic home run?"*

Post-Introductory Questions (After you have introduced someone to your business)

Note: These are a few super-smart "follow on" questions that will help lead you naturally to the next two steps in the Super-Smart Prospecting formula: MANAGING OBJECTIONS and CLOSING TO NEXT STEPS

> *"What did you like best about what you saw or heard?"*

> *"Do you see yourself as more of a product person, a business builder, or both?"*

> *"How much monthly cash flow would you like to create?"*

> *"Would you like to know the next steps?"*

> *"Is there anything else you need to know before you consider joining our team?"*

"On a scale of 1-10, with 1 being low, and 10 being high, how would you rate your overall interest level after seeing our presentation?"

"Is there anything else you need to know, or are you ready to get started?"

Important to remember: Don't forget to **be the messenger, not the message**. Your job is to simply introduce the tool (video, audio, webinar, etc.) by creating interest, excitement, and by getting the prospect's agreement to (1) review the tool, and (2) provide you with their feedback or comments.

So far you've learned how to CONNECT, QUALIFY, INVITE, and INTRODUCE. Now you are at the next step in the Super-Smart Prospecting Formula, and that is learning how to MANAGE OBJECTIONS.

5. MANAGE OBJECTIONS

I'm sure you noticed already that the previous chapter: "How To Be An Objections-Handling Ninja", was focused exclusively on learning the basics of how to manage objections, questions and concerns.

Why?

Because one of the biggest challenges for most network marketers – the one that stops so many from effective prospecting – is the fear of what to say or how to respond to people's questions or objections. Very simply put, it's the all-too-common fear of rejection.

Super-smart prospectors have learned to overcome any fear of addressing people's verbal challenges, objections or "negative energy-charged" questions.

If you haven't heard most of these yet, you soon will:

- *"I don't want to have to talk people into buying anything."*
- *"Is this one of those pyramids?"*
- *"If this is a network marketing scheme, I'm not interested."*
- *"Oh, those pyramid things never work."*
- *"Those products cost too much."*
- *"I'm way too busy…I don't have any time."*
- *"Only a few people ever make any money."*
- *"I don't like to sell – do I have to sell to be successful?"*
- *"Do you really think MLM is a good idea?"*

B.S. Also Stands For "Belief Systems"

Part of learning to manage objections is to understand that some of your prospect's fears, concerns or objections are legitimate, and some are based on their personal beliefs – even if they may be mistaken or misinformed beliefs.

We live in a "belief-driven universe" – people's beliefs are people's beliefs. Sometimes, no matter how hard you try, you may not be able to change or impact another person's beliefs.

Be very clear: It is NOT YOUR JOB to change people's beliefs. Most of the time the only belief system you CAN control or change is your OWN belief system.

Your REAL JOB is to accept the role of the "gentle detective" and to keep asking questions until you understand what a person needs, wants or doesn't want, and if possible offer them a solution that may solve their problem.

Sifting and Sorting: Another Name for Prospecting

Let's say I handed you a fifty-two-card deck of regular playing cards and gave you the following directions:

"Your job is to quickly look through the deck – in no more than 60 seconds – and find any card that is an ace, king or queen. Do not hand me a spade, heart or club. Follow those

directions and I'll give you one million dollars each for every card that meets that description!"

Would you sit there trying to figure out how much money you were going to make? Would you quit or get angry or disappointed, or would you get busy sifting and sorting through and handing me the Ace, King and Queen of Diamonds?

When working with people, your best "sorting tools" are a *curious mind*, *great questions*, a *willingness and intention to help them,* and the clear realization that you are not in the convincing or beliefs-changing business.

Your goal is to build a relationship, *find out what a person needs, wants or desires,* and if what you have is a reasonable solution, then introduce them to your solution and help them make a decision to buy, purchase, engage, or get involved.

Once you are capable of MANAGING OBJECTIONS, the rest of the steps in the Super-Smart Prospecting Formula start to fall into place naturally, and the entire communications process begins to flow.

So far you've learned how to CONNECT, QUALIFY, INVITE, INTRODUCE and MANAGE OBJECTIONS.

Next is one of the most misunderstood and underused steps – the CLOSE TO ACTION step.

6. CLOSE TO ACTION (or next steps)

Closing has been compared to fastening the last button of an overcoat. Why do so many people inadvertently miss that last button?

Assuming you've guided your prospect through the beginning steps of the formula: CONNECTING, QUALIFYING, INVITING, INTRODUCING, and MANAGING OBJECTIONS.

Then it should be easy to get to that last button.

Closing is about *clarity*. If you want clarity, ask closing questions. If you want to be a Super-Smart prospector and a skilled closer, ask better closing questions.

Closing is nothing more than "leading the communications" and helping people take the appropriate next steps. Closing is all about helping people clarify their thoughts and make decisions. When everyone is clear – then everyone can save time, energy and needless angst.

Closing is NOT trying to convince people; which doesn't work and doesn't serve anyone's best interests in the long term.

Here are some outstanding general questions you can ask following your introduction or after you've addressed initial objections. These questions are designed to help you understand what a person is thinking or feeling and help draw them into a conversation that clarifies issues or leads to decisions on the next steps.

> *"Deborah, after everything you've seen so far, do you see yourself as more of a product person, a business builder, or both?"*

> *"Bill, I'm eager to hear your impressions and feedback. What did you like best about the presentation?"*

Asking for a Decision

If for example, after one or more phone calls, and after you've managed a few objections or concerns, you could do a soft close by asking:

> *"Now that we seem to have covered most of the things you wanted to know about, are you ready to get started together?"*

> *"Jamie, based on all the information we've reviewed to this point, is there anything else you need to know before I explain how to get started?"*

> *"Marilyn, now that we're both clear on how important it is for you to start creating more cash flow for your family, would you like me to help you implement this?"*

> *"Tina, now that we've covered all your questions, my recommendation is that we get you enrolled in our system today … that way we can get your new business started immediately. Does that seem like a good plan to you?"*

Hint: Be sure you're prepared to outline the next steps if they say, "*Yes.*"

A slight variation is to summarize first, then close:

> *"Mary, you've had some great questions. With your personality and positive energy, I really feel we could build a profitable business together.*

> The CLOSE: *"Is there anything else you need to know OR are you ready to get started now?"*

If the person seems hesitant or you are not sure about their level of interest, then below are additional ways to discover what's holding them back.

Reluctance Closing Question

Sometimes people are hesitant and aren't even sure why. They may not know what to ask you. This is a great opportunity for you to help them with clarifying questions.

> *"Mary, I sense your interest, but at the same time I sense there is something holding you back. Is there something still unresolved in your mind?*

The "Scale of 1-to-10" Closing Question

This is an outstanding general question you can learn and use in a variety of situations to gauge your prospect's interest in your product or business offering.

A good way to start is by summing up or "prefacing".

> *"Jim, I really appreciate your interest and great questions. I'd really enjoy working with you and think we could build a successful business together..."*

> *"I have an important question.* (Then pause a moment*) On a scale of 1 to 10, if 1 is low and 10 is high, how would you rate your interest in moving forward and getting started?*

Hint: If they say anything less than a 5, you're probably wasting your time. If they respond with 6-7, here's what to say:

> *"Great! What else would you need from me or need to know to move you to a 9 or 10?*

If they respond with 8-10, here's what to say:

> *"Perfect, Jim. Let's get started. I'm excited about working with you. If you're like me you'll move to a 10 once you see what a great decision you've made"*

A Big Mistake: Not Closing At All

By far, the biggest prospecting mistake networkers make is not closing at all, especially when they've already done most of the work.

One study showed that nearly 70% of all presentations end without the presenter asking the prospect to make a decision. Apparently, many people are so afraid of rejection or losing a sale that they never get around to asking a closing question.

Don't waste all your preparation, your hard work or your valuable time by being afraid to ask closing questions. Refusal is not rejection. Prospects can never reject you. They can only reject what you are offering.

When you ready, ask your closing question and then stop. Be absolutely silent. Remind yourself, *"If I'm the first person to talk after I ask my closing question then I lose."*

Don't be afraid of the silence. Many sales are lost when you continue to talk, talk, and talk some more past the magic moment. You may have just talked your prospect out of the sale.

My Prospecting Mantra

Feel free to use it as a mental warm-up or an attitude check that can help you with your "closing mentality".

> *"I serve others by becoming a skilled closer and asking great questions. I serve others by helping them clarify what it is they need or want, and what steps are necessary so they can have what they need or want – I accept the reality that no matter how skilled I am or how wonderful my products or opportunities are, some people are going to be interested and some are not!"*

So far you've learned how to CONNECT – QUALIFY – INVITE – INTRODUCE – MANAGE OBJECTIONS – CLOSE TO ACTION.

The last step in the formula is one of the easiest to do and also one of the easiest to neglect, and that's the FOLLOW UP step.

7. FOLLOW UP

Following up the right way is one of the most important yet underused high leverage activities in prospecting communications; it is simply one of the very best ways to serve people and demonstrate professionalism.

FOCUSED FOLLOW UP is what network-marketing professionals do. It means having a **desired outcome** and a **focus point** for your "follow up conversation".

Research shows that almost 50% of sales people *never* follow up with a second contact, while another 25% make a second contact and stop.

Statistics also reveal that 80% of all sales are made on the fifth to twelfth contact. That means that **the vast majority of the time sales are lost due to lack of follow up**! In other words – there's a fortune to be made by learning to FOLLOW UP.

Following up is easy to do once you learn how – it's not difficult – but requires a little discipline and the right mindset.

There are three general objectives for following up:

1. Support the prospect in taking the next (agreed-upon) action step. (Examples could be; reviewing additional materials, trying your product, meeting your business partner, meeting their spouse, etc.)

2. To stay in touch with the prospect so you can be in a position to serve their needs if and when the opportunity arises.

3. Provide additional services or products after the sale of your product, service or opportunity; to strengthen and build the relationship.

Don't just follow up – follow up with a purpose – an objective. Clearly identify the reason for the communication and your intended outcome. Being focused means you have an outcome in mind and a specific reason for following up.

Share (or remind) the person the reason for your follow up.

Good Reasons for Following Up

1. To remind someone of the time and directions for a meeting, introductory presentation or phone call.

2. To get a person's feedback and determine interest after they've reviewed a tool or sampled or experienced your product.

3. To reconnect and evaluate if the timing is better for them to try your product or review your business opportunity. To provide important product or business updates.

4. To determine if a person needs any additional information or has questions before they get started.

5. To demonstrate that the relationship is important to you; you care about their needs; to learn if you can continue to help them with your product or service.

Follow Up Questions

To set and agree on a meeting time:

> *"Dr. Wilson, last month you suggested I should get back with you at this time to see if your schedule had lightened up …would now be a better time to (…meet my business partner …attend my business mixer …meet me for coffee?")*

> *"Mary, you suggested I contact you once you got back from your vacation. Are you free for a few minutes this Tuesday night, or would next Tuesday be better for you?"*

To gain someone's feedback and opinion:

> *"Dave, you had a look at our streaming video yesterday. I really value your feedback and opinion. What did you like best? Was there anything in particular that caught your attention?"*

> *"Hi Penny, I sent you the information you requested, plus the link to our company website. Do you have a few minutes to share your initial impressions?"*

To build the relationship and keep your promise:

> *"Suzanne, it's been several months since we spoke about my new business, and I promised to give you a progress report. I really think you're going to enjoy hearing the news. Do you have a few minutes for a quick update?"*

> *"Hi Evelyn. You've been trying our product for over a month now. I'm really eager to get your impressions. What have you noticed? ...What do you like best?"*

To provide service:

> *"We just launched a new product (or service) and I thought you'd appreciate learning about what it's doing for people. Can I send you over some information or a link to a video overview?"*

> *"The last time we spoke, you were reluctant to get involved because the timing was off for you and you were experiencing some challenges. Would you have a few minutes for a quick update?"*

Skillful follow up can create some surprising results – even when you initially thought a person wasn't interested. Whether you're trying to rekindle someone's interest or keep a customer after the sale – so practice *focused follow up*.

Let people know you care.

James Bond and the Super-Smart Prospecting Formula

For some people, learning and internalizing a "seven-step" model may seem difficult at first. I want to encourage AND promise you that it's easier than you think.

If you are willing take the time to learn the model and add it to your skill set, it will pay huge, positive dividends.

Now, if you've ever seen a James Bond movie, whether you noticed or not, you've probably observed James Bond employing the super-smart prospecting strategy.

Let's set the scene:

James is having a drink at the casino bar in Monte Carlo. He observes an attractive girl moving slowly in her seat to sound of the orchestra. James saunters over for a little chat.

James **connecting**: *"You look like you're having a great time there … all by yourself. I've been watching you. You are absolutely breathtaking."*

Girl: *"Thank you. I love this music."*

James **qualifying**: *"Did you say you're here all by yourself?"*

Girl: *"No I didn't say, but for some reason my friend is very late."*

James **inviting**: *"While you're waiting, could I offer you a drink and some fascinating conversation?"*

Girl: *"Fascinating? What if my friend turns up? He might not … understand."*

James **managing objections**: *"Well, if he does turn up, I'll tell him I'm the official casino ambassador in charge of making sure the natives don't bother the tourists."*

Girl: *"O.K. then, I'll have a dirty martini, straight up."*

James **introducing**: *"Great choice. How about we take our drinks and go out for a leisurely stroll on the beach? There's a beautiful full moon and something I want you to see."*

Girl: *"No, I can't. I have to leave in just a few minutes. … It's complicated."*

James **managing objections** and **closing to action**: *"I understand complicated. What do you say if we have breakfast in the morning by the pool? Breakfast is not complicated. Nine am - I'll be waiting."*

Girl: *"All right Mr. Bond … just breakfast."*

James **following up**: *"Just one more thing. Would you please set the alarm on your phone for 8 am? I don't like to be kept waiting … even by a beautiful girl. O.K?"*

Girl: *"Oh, all right James, I'll set my alarm for 8 am and see you in the morning."*

Notice anything? First, in this dialogue, James never did introduce himself. Not his usual, "*I'm Bond, James Bond.*" So even double 07 isn't perfect. He left something out but still managed to make positive forward progress.

After all he doesn't need to tell a person, even a beautiful girl, **everything** on their first connection.

Obviously the girl is NOT telling James everything either, because she somehow knew his name even though he didn't mention it. She's holding something back – and often your prospects will hold something back even if you ask all the right questions.

Second, and most important, **James followed the super smart formula almost to the letter**.

He began by **connecting**, then **qualifying**, **inviting**, **introducing** (an idea), **managing objections, closing** and then **following up**.

Anyone, even James Bond, who prefers to do things his own way, can follow a simple seven-step formula. Make that double 07!

CONNECT
QUALIFY
INVITE
INTRODUCE
MANAGE OBJECTIONS
CLOSE TO ACTION
FOLLOW UP

With just a few hours of practice, you will start to get more comfortable and proficient. Once that happens, prospecting starts to become fun, and your effectiveness (and results) will grow impressively.

Enjoy!

Monte Taylor, Jr.

CHAPTER SIX

Bonus Prospecting and Persuasion Nuggets

In twenty-five-plus years I've been exposed to a wide variety of interesting prospecting tips, closing techniques and persuasive communication strategies in direct selling,

In this chapter I want to share a few that have been especially useful, and encourage you to give each a try – and see if they work as well for you as they have for me and many others.

This first nugget is an "oldie but goodie" and I touched on it briefly in Chapter Three. Some of these oldies are also the most valuable because they're based on enduring, time-tested human principals that work again and again.

It's an easy-to-use tool – and very handy when you want to gain a better sense of a prospect's overall interest level.

My Favorite Closing Question

Several months ago, my son Eric phoned me and said, *"Dad, one of my biggest challenges is to know what to say after I have made a presentation to a prospect. Sometimes I don't feel I am a good closer. Do you have any ideas that could help me?"*

This is the principle I shared with Eric.

For decades, talk show hosts and magazines have featured "lists and rankings" as a human interest, attention-getting staple – simply because people respond positively to classifying or ranking almost anything you can imagine.

97

You've seen lists and headlines like these:

> "The ten most effective way to please your boss, friend or lover"

> "The top five family vacation beaches in the world"

> "The seven things you should never eat when you want to lose weight fast"

> "Four things you should never tell an absolute stranger"

> "Five questions you should always ask before you propose marriage to anyone"

So how can you borrow on the power of human nature?

Once you have made any presentation or shared your story, the next step is getting your prospect to tell you what they are thinking; what is on their mind; what, if anything, is keeping them from making a decision or moving forward. Are they interested, intrigued, confused – or what?

Here's an answer for you.

The "Scale of One-to-Ten" Question

This question sounds simple, and IT IS simple, but very, very powerful.

A good way to start the "scale of one-to-ten question" is by summing up or prefacing. Here is an example:

> You: *"Jim, I really appreciate your interest and great questions. I would really enjoy working with you, and I think we could build a great business together."*

Now here is your scale of one-to-ten closing question:

You: *"I have an important question,"* (and then pause for a moment)

"Jim, on a scale of one to ten, if one is low and ten is high, how would you rate your interest in moving forward and getting started?"

Hint: If Jim says anything less than a five, you are probably wasting your time. If he responds with a six or a seven, here is what to say:

You: "Great. What else would you need from me or need to know to move you to a nine or a ten?"

That is a great question. Listen to what he says and address his concern using AVVIS. If Jim responds with eight or ten, here's what to say:

You: *"Perfect! I'm really excited about working with you …and if you're like me, you will get to a ten once you see what a great decision you have made." "Shall we get started?"*

With this question you are creating a soft, easy, non-confrontational way to get your prospect to open up and tell you what they're thinking. It works like magic.

"Hey, Jim. On a scale of one to ten, with one being low, and ten being high, where do you find yourself right now? Tell me how you feel."

What you are really looking for is if there are any roadblocks. You are offering them a way to get problems or concerns on the table. When issues are clear and in the open, you have a chance to deal with anything that is keeping them from moving forward.

Back to Eric's Question

By the way, as it turns out, a few weeks later Eric asked me to attend a small-group presentation he was holding for a few prospects. After the presentation, he privately asked each of his prospects the "scale of one-to-ten question".

Several of his prospects said, *"I'm a nine," or "I'm a ten."* And Eric said, *"Great. Let's get together now for a moment and make plans to get started. I am really excited about working with you."*

The good news was that by asking prospects the scale-of-one-to-ten question, Eric learned which prospects were ready to get started, and which prospects needed more information or had concerns they needed to address; he knew exactly where and how to focus his energies.

The Secret to Finding Eagles in a Flock of Turkeys

I'm sure you'd agree that most network marketers are substantially more interested in finding a few eagles that soar rather than having to wade through acres of time-wasting turkeys that flap around making lots of...well, noise.

Of course, when it comes to birds, it's easy to tell the difference – just look. Unfortunately, when it comes to humans, it's a much more challenging task.

Of course, I don't mean any disrespect for anyone. My point is simply that many network marketers spend enormous amounts of time and energy trying to engage the wrong people.

Who are the wrong people? Those are the people who have little or no interest in your product, service or opportunity.

While the following story isn't specifically related to engaging opt-in leads, I believe it helps makes the point.

Just recently I was asked to have a brief in-person meeting with a couple I didn't know. Some business partners who felt the couple might be good prospects for our business project had arranged the meeting.

Immediately after meeting, saying hello and sitting down with the couple, the gentleman across from me asked, *"So what's this all about?"*

Of course I realized right away that he was asking me to bottom line my presentation quickly so he could respond with a, "yea" or "nay." His demeanor suggested he was pretty much already at "nay."

Pausing for a moment, I said this: *"I'd be happy to tell you about me and what I'm up to, but I'm really very interested in hearing about the two of you. Please tell me how you met."*

So he and his friend proceeded to share their story. I continued to say, *"Oh, very interesting. Please tell me more."*

With just a few minutes of questioning and listening, I soon realized the couple were there to tell me all about THEIR business opportunity, and frankly weren't interested in learning much about anything else.

That's okay – this is not a huge problem – nor does it make anyone a turkey. It's fun to meet new and interesting people. However, spending lots of time presenting or talking, given the facts of this situation was a real time waster – which is the real turkey.

So here's **the secret** to telling the difference between eagles and turkeys:

Keep control of the conversation and ask great questions!

Take the lead and recognize one of the most important things you need to know: "Is the person I'm speaking with a

prospect, or in reality just a **suspect**, and how can I quickly find out?

Here's how to tell the difference: Suspects ARE NOT qualified. Prospects ARE qualified.

Although we covered this in the Super-Smart Prospecting section under QUALIFY, I hope you don't mind a recap and review because qualifying will save you gobs and gobs of time and wasted energy. Qualifying will help clarify when and where it's time to apply your energy.

How do you know which is which? Qualify people by asking great questions. A suspect is someone you haven't qualified in terms of need or desire. You have little or no idea if they might want or need what you have to offer. You might think they need it, but you haven't confirmed that by asking great questions.

A prospect is someone YOU HAVE qualified. This person has shared enough information with you so you can determine that they indeed qualify for an invitation to review whatever it is you have to offer.

Let me make a suggestion: Sit down and write out some qualifying questions that work for your product, service or opportunity.

Here are some examples, and then I'll share one of my favorites:

> *"Bill, I understand you filled out a form saying you might be open to learning about a side project …tell me, how things are going with your career right now?"*
>
> *"Sam, you responded by saying you might be open to learning about a part-time income project …so tell me, first, how is the economy affecting your business?"*

"Tom, you filled out a form saying you might be open to learning a home business project ...tell me, what, if anything, have you done in the past to protect yourself with a Plan B?"

If the person you are speaking to answers your question, shares a problem or a real need, then you can proceed with the invitation to look at what you have to offer.

Don't forget, whenever someone tries to take over the lead by asking you to "quickly tell them about your business," turn the tables, take the lead back by saying something like this:

"Oh thanks, I'd love to. But first I'd really enjoy hearing a little bit about you and what you're working on or excited about right now."

Now, I promised to share one of my favorite qualifying conversations. It goes like this:

"Mary, how interesting would it be for you right now if you could have a project that made money for you while you sleep?"

If they respond with, *"Well, what kind of project?"* Say this:

You: *Of course I'll tell you all about it, but here's the real question – if there was something that had the potential to make money for you while you sleep, would you invest 15 minutes to learn more about it?"*

And if they respond, *"Yes, that could be interesting."* Or, *"Yes, tell me more."* Now you have a real **prospect** – and you can invite them to take a serious look at what you have to offer.

A "Dream Forward" Exercise That Works Like Magic!

This is a short exercise that works wonders for creating positive, eye-opening conversations, and engaging and involving prospects.

It's designed to help your audience (or prospect) imagine what it would be like to have a consistent and dependable monthly residual income stream that covered all their living expenses.

Here's what I say to introduce the exercise:

> *"Think about your financial freedom number for just a moment."*

Or, in a one-on-one situation or phone conversation, I'll ask this:

> *"I'm curious, Bill, have you ever thought about your financial freedom number?"*

Of course, most people don't know exactly what I mean at first, so I explain further:

> *"Please take a moment to think about how much money you need coming into your checking or savings account automatically every month, year in and year out, to cover every expense you have. Everything! Then add another 30% on top for any extras such as savings, vacations or rainy days."*

To keep things moving, I'll offer an example.

> *"Let's say you need $10,000 to cover all your monthly expenses. Add an additional 30%, which is $3,000. If you add those together your financial freedom number is $13,000 a month."*

> *"Now that you've had a moment to think about it, what's your financial freedom number?"*

You can use this exercise in large and small presentations, home business mixers and one-on -one presentations.

Remember, **never ever promise people or guarantee they can achieve their number**.

But offer this instead:

> *"Bill, if you have a genuine desire for change in your life, and you're willing to put forth the effort, then just imagine if in the next few years, working together, we could achieve your number."*
>
> *"Imagine if you could join the tens of thousands of networking professionals that are earning full-time incomes with part-time effort. Bill, what would you say?"*

This exercise almost never fails to create a positive buzz and get people thinking and dreaming and asking:

> *"What would I have to do to achieve my number?*

Which, by the way, is an important conversation you want to have with people.

Be prepared to show people what kind of time, energy and dedication would be required; how many customers and distributors creating how much sales volume would be necessary (using your company data) for them to reach their number.

Try it – it can open up some very interesting conversations and discussions with people.

Seven Positive Emotional Triggers: INSBYYL

You are probably wondering what on earth **INSBYYL** means. What it means is (I'm embarrassed to report) that thus far I haven't been able to come up with a good acronym for the following seven words and phrases:

- **I**magine
- **N**o Excuses
- The **S**imple Truth
- **B**elieve In Better
- **Y**ou Deserve
- **Y**ou Decide
- **L**et's Get Started

These words and phrases represent seven ideals, or what I'll call "positive emotional triggers", that were identified after years of research by one of the world's most talented communications experts, Dr. Frank Luntz.

In his thought-provoking book, *Words That Work*, *It's Not What You Say, It's What People Hear,* Luntz offers a behind-the-scenes look at how the tactical use of words and phrases can affect what we buy, whom we vote for, and even what we believe in.

These are conceptual ideals that not only resonate with people, but also, if used appropriately, can help you move some people out of their head and in to their heart.

Luntz also wrote, *What Americans Really Want …Really*, plus, *Win: The Key Principles to Take Your Business from Ordinary to Extraordinary.*

After reading and enjoying all three of his books, I wanted to borrow some of the more powerful ideas, (and ideals), seven of which I felt might be useful at appropriate times, for richer and perhaps more effective communications.

Notice I occasionally found opportunities to weave some of these rich and meaningful concepts into the language of my scripts.

> *"Mary, just **imagine** if in the next few years, by working together, we could achieve your number."*

> *"**Imagine** if you could join the tens of thousands of networking professionals that are earning full-time incomes with part-time effort. Bill, what would you say?"*

> *"Monte, **the simple truth** is that no one can guarantee how quickly you'll reach your income goals with your new business. I can only guarantee that I'll do my very best to help you every step of the way."*

> *"Dave, Let's take a look at the presentation together, and then we'll go over the small start-up costs – then **you decide**. **You deserve** to see what this is all about and **decide** if it's right for you.*

> *"Jim, is there anything else you need to know; or would you like to know the next steps and how we can **get started** together now?" If not, **let's get started**.*

If you happen to watch Dr. Phil on T.V., notice how often he sums up his thoughts or recommendations to guests by saying, "**You decide**." Or, "**You deserve** to know what this is all about." "**You decide** if this is something you no longer want in your life."

I've realized, especially after studying authors such as Luntz, or Cialdini (*Influence, The Psychology of Persuasion*) or Beckwith (*Selling the Invisible*) that there is a learnable, natural, underlying psychology to better communications with people.

People respond well to certain basic ideals such as, "you decide for yourself" or "you deserve better" or "you deserve to know all the details before make up your mind."

If you are willing to pay attention and learn, you can absolutely improve your ability to persuade or appropriately influence others. Each of us has the potential for increased rapport and positive influence.

I'd encourage you to begin reading and studying the authors and speakers who focus on sharing ideas for scientifically-based people communications. I have some suggestions for you at the end of this book.

Always be asking yourself, "How can I appropriately use this concept, these words or phrases, to give my message a better chance of resonating and connecting with people?"

Most people, I believe, want to know and hear, **the simple truth**. Not a convoluted story that begins with "the dance of the seven veils" or a smarmy, snappy comeback to their question or objection.

Be your prospect's thoughtful guide, their Sherpa, their concierge. Be interested. Listen. Be a super-smart communicator. Be a relationship engineer – build better relationships.

Strive for more clarity in your conversations; **no excuses**. Take the conversational lead and help people discover and find what they want and need.

Believe in better – I know I do.

Now that you've learned what to say, how to engage and close opt-in prospects, and even your warm market contacts, **imagine** all the possibilities for increased success with your direct selling or network marketing business.

You're ready – so **let's get started**.

How to Keep Improving Your Skills

Free Videos And Audios Linked To This Book!!!

I hope you take advantage of "**Let's Make Prospecting Easy**," my free weekly audio blog, where I offer ongoing prospecting, communication, networking, persuasion and business building tips just for you – it's available exclusively to subscribers.

As a subscriber, you also get exclusive access to FREE streaming videos – designed to help you get full value from this book. Please click or go to the link below to subscribe:

www.montetaylor.com/profitwithleads-free

Here are just a few examples of subscriber feedback:

"Wow, Monte! This has to be one of the most simple and enjoyable suggestions you have shared yet! Just thinking about applying it to some situations that have felt "heavy" to me immediately lifted the weight and I'm looking forward to challenging myself with it in oh so many ways. I'll keep you posted as I use it more and more."

"I am so grateful that you share your words of wisdom with us Monte. Thank you so much for helping me to keep all things in perspective."

"… Thanks for your audio posts Monte – I learned a long time ago being grateful is not hard to do. … People deserve any and all consideration we can give them, I always ask myself: What does it hurt to be grateful or thankful? What it I was the

only person who acknowledged their worth that day? What if my comment was something that turned a bad day into a WOW DAY? Don't we all deserve to have WOW DAYS?"

Recommended Reading and Further Study

Here is a list of just a few of my favorites based on authors that I found myself rereading:

"No B.S Direct Marketing" - Dan S. Kennedy (any book by D. Kennedy)

"Words That Work" - Dr. Frank Luntz (any book by F. Luntz)

"Inspired Marketing" - Dr. Joe Vitale (any book by J. Vitale)

"Influencing With Integrity" - Genie Z. Laborde

"Getting Everything You Can Out Of All You Got" - Jay Abraham

"Selling the Invisible" - Harry Beckwith, Jr.

"The Compound Effect" - Darrin Hardy

"The Psychology of Influence" - Robert B. Cialdini

"The 22 Immutable Laws of Marketing" - Al Reis/Jack Trout

"The Articulate Executive" - Granville Toogood

"The 21 Irrefutable Laws of Leadership" - John C. Maxwell

"Little Things Matter" - Todd Smith

"The War of Art" - Steven Pressfield

One of my all-time favorite books, not focused on marketing or communications, but offering acres of worthwhile perspective on the human experience and what motivates others is, *"What Really Matters"* – Tony Schwartz

Finally, if you'd like to connect, need additional information, have any thoughts, questions, comments, a recommendation or even a story you'd like to share, please feel free to contact me through my website: www.montetaylor.com

To Your Great Success!

Monte Taylor, Jr.

Monte Taylor, Jr.

Praise for Objections Handled!
101 Sample Scripts for Network Marketers – Learn To Say The Right Thing To Every Prospect

"Phenomenal Tips"

I absolutely loved this book. It gave me the confidence to go out there and utilize everything this book showed me to go talk to more people. I feel I am going to accomplish everything that I desire and I found myself living my dreams. I am blessed and fortunate that Monte created this book for us who have the courage to do what we truly want. - JFII

"Great Read! Great Info!"

I've been in sales for years and understand the value-scripted rebuttals. This book does so much more! The power of Monte`s formulas makes prospecting fairly easy! Great read!! - Todd Robinson

"Must Read"

This is by far one of the best books that I've read in regards to Network Marketing. I purchased this book expecting to receive some sample scripts that could come in useful for handling various objections, but instead what I received was a training guide that goes deep into detail on the mindset of prospecting. I've recommended this book to everybody on my team and I will continue to do so because it is THAT good! This book is along the lines of "Go Pro," by Eric Worre, in terms of helpfulness but I actually think that [Objections Handled] is an even more effective training tool. - Jay

"An Excellent Guide"

Being deaf, I can't hear the CDs that everyone else can use as part of their learning. So I have to read books and some of them take a long time to be read.

This book is what I have been missing - and believe me, am starving for. (Hint to the author!) I want to actually read conversational scripts from start to finish so I can comprehend how to control a conversation. Even if it comes to a dead end, I can watch and learn with words on paper how it all works. - Christine Kerr

"Thoughtful, Practical, True!"

Not only has Monte done it all – from building in the field to managing in corporate – but he has a sensitivity to the issues that most confound, confuse, and defeat direct sellers. As a result, "Objections Handled" provides the resources and insights direct sellers need to overcome apprehensions and to conquer the shortfalls of inexperience and uncertainty. And for experienced network marketers, it's a superior way to remind and rethink one's business practices. Like Monte, this book is practical, thoughtful, and true! - Clifton Jolly, PhD

"Tough Situations Handled"

Great book but it's more than just dealing with objections. Monte tiers the content in manner that builds on precepts. He doesn't just throw scripts at you; he builds a foundation on the psychology behind why the tactics work so well. If the book stopped at just at the content in the mindset section (chapter one) it would still be an enormous help to many, it was to me. That said, it doesn't stop there, instead it launches from this base into very practical formulas and strategies for prospecting and dealing with objections (chapters two and three). If that wasn't enough, Monte goes into detail on specific objections that I think the reader would find invaluable for "how to". I'm not in the networking industry and I say that, as you don't need to be a network marketer to benefit from this book.

All of us sell in some way or another; we have to sell ourselves to our employers, employees, customers and friends for many reasons including causes we may believe in and goals we want to achieve that involve collaboration. When we do we will sometimes face resistance in the form of objections. Knowing how to face these objections head on without being discouraged when we encounter them is a big reason to buy this book. - L. Weeks

"Gotta Get It!"

If you are serious about building a network marketing business, this book is a MUST

Of all the books I have read over the years pertaining to building a network marketing business, this is the most concise and easy to actually use in the everyday building of your business. Thank you Monte for sharing this information with us. - Tina Myers

"Clear, Concise, Entertaining"

Monte hits a home run on this one. He covers the bases in a very fast read. I have already tried several of his techniques with sweet success. I would recommend this book to anyone who really wants to capture a piece of the passive income available to all of us. - F. Okubo

"Simplicity Works"

I love Monte's style of writing because he communicates in a way that says simple is better. And since I'm famous for trying to reinvent the wheel, this is the kind of book that helps give me confidence that I can follow a simple script that feels authentic to me. This book is an easy 5 star! - Brent Abel

"Phenomenal Tips"

I absolutely loved this book. It gave me the confidence to go out there and utilize everything this book showed me to go talk to more people. I feel I am going to accomplish everything that I desire and I found myself living my dreams. I am blessed and fortunate that Monte created this book for us who have the courage to do what we truly want. - JFII

www.ingramcontent.com/pod-product-compliance
Lightning Source LLC
Chambersburg PA
CBHW071800200526
45167CB00017B/715